DANCE AND GENDER

Choreography and Dance
1998, Vol. 5, Part 1, pp. iii–iv
Photocopying permitted by license only

Contents

Choreography and Dance
1998, Vol. 5, Part 1, pp. 1–7
Photocopying permitted by license only

If All the World's a Stage, I Want Better Lighting: Engendering Dance/Engendering Knowledge

Kim Grover-Haskin

If the dance work is a symbolic world and each symbolic world is created from a particular perspective or world view, what kind of symbolic world emerges from a feminist world view? (Goodman, 1978, p. 1) Gender is the issue central to this question. A feminist theoretical lens focusing on dance scrutinizes the dance experience through the world view of gender. This feminist world view becomes prominent in the making, experiencing, and perceiving of the dance work as a specific gendered reality, a reality which constructs and enfolds the dance work. It is my intention to discuss this phenomenon and analyze Twyla Tharp's *Nine Sinatra Songs* based on the components of liberal feminist thought and gender.

KEY WORDS   Feminist theory, gender, *Nine Sinatra Songs*, world view, liberal feminism.

In December of 1992 I had the experience of a lifetime. I took my doctoral exams. It was out of these exams that I formulated an idea about the artistic practice of dance and feminism. I happened upon Nelson Goodman's (1978) *Ways of Worldmaking* in which he develops an aesthetic perspective for the visual arts. After reading Goodman's book, I asked myself: If the dance work is a symbolic world and each symbolic world is created from a particular perspective or world view, what kind of symbolic world emerges from a woman choreographer's world view?

This question became a point of inquiry for me to investigate the intersection of gender and dance. In 1994, the annual conference of the Congress on Research in Dance, Engendering Dance/Engendering

Knowledge: Dance, Gender, and Interdisciplinary Dialogues in the Arts, focused on how gender impacted the dance discipline. It brought together a body of scholars to discourse about dance and gender in research, pedagogy, history, somatics, performance, education, anthropology, and much more. The conference provided individuals an arena in which to reflect critically upon the world and their world views.

The following papers in this issue of *Choreography and Dance* are critical reflections from that conference. Through lenses of personal insight or public scrutiny, each author examines the experiences of women, and men, in the dance world. This is fundamental to engendering dance/engendering knowledge because it is only through these experiences that knowledge is revealed and different perspectives are embraced. My particular focus is upon feminist theory and dance.

Dance scholars use feminist analysis as a lens through which the dance experience is viewed and re-viewed. Such a lens, when applied to dance, focuses on the multifaceted aspects of the dance experience via a woman-centered perspective or world view. Feminist theories explore, describe, and explain these world views through sociological and philosophical tenets. Dance provides the medium for these world views to be voiced.

The dance work is a symbolic site/sight for creating meaning among dance, dancer, and audience socially, politically, and culturally. Creating the dance work reveals the world view at work in its shaping and forming. Performing the dance work is an unique experience enhancing perceptual and cognitive awareness of self and world. The performance extends to an audience—stimulating aesthetic and perceptual realms of understanding and appreciation to enhance new worlds or visions. Since the dance work represents a symbolic world conceived and shaped through personal, social, and political world views, feminist theories help to explain these world views.

Feminist theories examine social and political factors at work in shaping the experience of everyday life. A feminist theoretical lens focusing on dance scrutinizes the dance experience through the world view of gender. This feminist world view becomes prominent in the making, experiencing, and perceiving of the dance work because the world view delineates a specific gendered reality, a reality which constructs and enfolds the dance from its inception to its final presentation.

By applying feminist theories to dance, feminist world views become prominent in how the dance formulates and is formulated by gender. Gender is an element which must be considered in the how the dance work is conceived, performed, and received. There are many feminist theories which explain how gender impacts our everyday lives. I have chosen to focus on liberal feminist theory. If the dance work is a symbolic world and each symbolic world is created from a particular perspective or world view, what kind of dance emerges from a liberal feminist world view?

Feminism is an opportunity to examine "the content of our world view as well as the modes of knowing and communication that provides its basis" (Oliver and Gershman, 1989, p. 30). It provides an avenue for re-viewing dance. A liberal feminist proposes an unique perspective. In order to analyze this perspective and its relevance to engendering dance/engendering knowledge, liberal feminist theory must be explained and related to a dance performance experience.

Liberal Feminism: Everyone Should Have a Shot at the Bolshoi

Liberal feminism is rooted in the historical era of the Enlightenment in which values such as independence, equal opportunity, and individualism were encouraged. Patriarchal proponents of these values were John Locke and J.J. Rousseau. Founded on the idea of natural rights, the public/private dispute is central to its political stance. Natural rights were premised on the definition of a world based on rationality. As Donovan (1992, p. 2) states:

As in the ancient Stoic view, the world was seen to work rationally according to mathematical, "natural" laws. Each individual had access, autarchically, to these laws, because each individual had a God-given rational faculty.

What liberalism failed to include was the subjective realm of experience, experience which was not always governed by reason. The rational took precedence over the non-rational, a category to which women were often relegated. The advent of the industrial revolution brought about a prominent demarcation between public and private spheres. "The public world of work became split off from the private world of the home as never before" (Donovan, p. 3). Early proponents of liberal feminism include Abigail Adams who, during the

Revolutionary War, emphasized *Remember the Ladies*, Judith Sargent Murray who published *On Equality of the Sexes* in 1790 and Mary Wollstonecraft completing her work entitled *A Vindication of the Rights of Woman* in January of 1792 (Donovan, p. 1).

In the nineteenth century, liberal feminism began its discourse through the works of Elizabeth Cady Stanton and Susan B. Anthony. Stanton and Anthony challenged the foundation that defined women as irrational. Stanton states, "... nothing adds such dignity to character as the recognition of one's self-sovereignty; the right to an equal place, everywhere conceded—a place earned by personal merit" (Donovan, p. 19).

African American women were also striving for equality though their struggle was often centered around issues of race. As Stanton and Anthony forged ahead to gain the vote for women and African American men, African American women were invisible. Activists such as Sojourner Truth, Sarah Grimke, and Ida B. Wells focused on bringing visibility to African American women. They pronounced a liberal platform battling not only a system of inequities against women, but against a white women's movement as well.

Through this historical foundation of liberal thought and values, liberal feminism emerges. Seminal to liberal feminism is the assertion that characteristics of family or race are not innately oppressive or inferior but are made so. Alison Jaggar (1984, p. 84) states "... each individual should be able to rise in society just as far as his or her talents permit, unhindered by restraints of law or custom."

It is a matter of opportunity, not of ascribed gender roles, race, or class. The system is unfair if a woman's opportunity is not equal. For example, if a woman asks in her ballroom dance class, "Why does the boy always have to lead? It seems to me the better dancer should lead." (N.O.W. News, 1978, p. 1). She objectively assesses the situation in relation to her abilities. She is positing what Belenky *et al.* (1986, p. 99) defines as procedural knowledge.

Procedural knowers are practical pragmatic problem solvers. Far from will-o-wisps, their feet are planted firmly on the ground. They are trying with more or less success, to take control of their lives in a planned, deliberate fashion.

Thus, women recognize their selves in relation to an inequality. They voice their opinions accordingly, in relation to that inequality, but they do not detach their identities from its external aspects. Belenky *et al.* (1986, p. 129) states, "Procedural knowers feel like chameleons; they cannot help but take on the color of any structure they inhabit." Therefore, liberal feminists voice reaction to an inequity in a system they are not necessarily interested in changing. Instead they want to re-shape it.

To apply this to dance, liberal feminists would acknowledge that "Everyone Should Have a Shot at the Bolshoi." Everyone should have the opportunity via education and training to legitimately acquire that goal. If the Bolshoi does not provide this opportunity, feminists would react to implement change within it. The Bolshoi would remain intact but its traditions would be challenged and re-shaped.

Choreographing from a liberal world view embodies reaction with decisions that evolve in contrast to standards and conventions yet remain tied to the system from which they originated. One good example is Twyla Tharp's *Nine Sinatra Songs*.

In *Nine Sinatra Songs* Tharp manipulates the ballroom dance convention. The first three dances in the work are duets to favorite Sinatra songs, *Softly as I Leave You, Strangers in the Night*, and *One for My Baby*. Two couples perform to *My Way* in the fourth piece which is followed again by three more duets to *Somethin' Stupid, All the Way*, and *Forget Domani*. The finale is a reprise of *My Way* with all the dancers assembled on stage. Each duet is unique with moods ranging from light hearted, to somber, and romantic.

Throughout *Nine Sinatra Songs*, Tharp maintains the ballroom form, but manipulates it into a performing experience which is presentational rather than social. Her use of a theatrical stage and virtuosic dancers promotes a re-evaluation of convention while, at the same time, playing with it.

When I watch the dancers in *Nine Sinatra Songs*, a great virtuosity and technical prowess is evident. The body becomes a device that is presented for display and, as such, in its virtuosic nature becomes a visual spectacle. In her analysis of *Nine Sinatra Songs* Susan Foster (1985, p. 63) states:

The viewer is presented with glossy, impenetrable objects. Their craft delights; the technical prowess of the dancers is admirable; the witty puns and remarks on dance serve to unite the audience as members of an "in-group"-who prefer well-crafted rebellion to more conventional forms of dance such as the ballet (p. 63).

In other words, the body is used as a spectacle, an object of consumption for viewers. The viewer is visually satisfied with its presentation.

Twyla Tharp presents the convention and constraints of ballroom dance. She chooses dancers who are described as classically trained and technically brilliant, and utilizes the traditional theatrical stage as a showcase for their talents. The dancers' performance is all encompassing, enticing the audience into a viewing experience which is satisfying. *Nine Sinatra Songs* maintains the status quo of women in the ballroom genre: beautiful, and partnered. Laura Jacobs (1992, p. 6) states:

> You can understand such handling in *Nine Sinatra Songs*, a dance that reads as social history and social criticism—it is simultaneously brilliantly, factual, sentimental, and sarcastic. Even though the women come forward as beauties…and despite Stacy Caddell's hilarious, swooping style in "Something Stupid," a memorable instance when a full-bodied female warmth and character floods the stage, *Nine Sinatra Songs* is still the men's show. The women are silken ciphers, bent and twirled and twined into cupolas and gewgaws—ivy around oak.

Tharp's *Nine Sinatra Songs* instills a sense of reaction to underlying frames or conventions but does not seek to change them. Essentially, they remain intact. Belenky *et al.* (1986, p. 127) makes this connection to liberal feminists as procedural knowers.

> Women who rely on procedural knowledge are systematic thinkers in more than one sense of the term. Their thinking is encapsulated within systems. They can criticize a system, but only in the system's terms, only according to the system's standards… If, for example, they are feminists, they want equal opportunities for women within the capitalistic structure; they do not question the premises of the structure. When these women speak of "beating the system," they do not mean violating its expectations but rather exceeding them.

In conclusion, everyone should have a shot at the Bolshoi. The question is, will the Bolshoi provide the opportunity?

References

Acocella, J. (1992). Twyla Tharp: Divided loyalties. *Art in America*, **80**(5), 59–61.
Belenky, M.F., Clinchy, B.M., Goldberger, N.R. and Tarule, J.M. (1986). *Women's Ways of Knowing*. New York: Basic Books, Inc.
Chafetz, J.S. (1988). *Feminist Sociology: An Overview of Contemporary Theories*. Itasca, Ill: F.E. Peacock Publishers, Inc.
Donovan, J. (1992). *Feminist theory: The Intellectual Traditions of American Feminism*. (Expanded Edition) New York: Frederick Ungar Publishing Co., Inc.
Foster, S. (1985). The signifying body: Reaction and resistance in postmodern dance. *Theatre Journal*, **37**(1), 45–64.
Goodman, N. (1978). *Ways of Worldmaking*. Indianapolis, IN: Hackett Publishing Co.

Hardy, C. (April, 1992). Brief brilliant phoenix, Twyla Tharp and dancers. *The World and I, 7*(4), 146–152.

Jacobs, L. (January–March, 1992). Role model. *The New Dance Review.* 4(3), 3–6.

Jaggar, A.M. and Rothenberg, P.S. (1984). *Feminist Frameworks* (2nd ed.). New York: McGraw-Hill book company.

Meisner, N. (November 1, 1992). Come dance with me. *Dance and Dancers.* 12–16.

N.O.W. News, Bay Area Chapter. (June, 1978). 6(6), 1.

Oliver, D. with Gershman, K.W. (1989). *Education, Modernity, and Fractured Meaning: Toward a Process Theory of Teaching and Learning.* Albany, New York: State University of New York Press.

Stacey, J. (1993). Untangling feminist theory. In D. Richardson and V. Robinson (Eds.), *Thinking Feminist: Key Concepts in Women's Studies* (pp. 49–73). New York: The Guilford Press.

Choreography and Dance
1998, Vol. 5, Part 1, pp. 9–23
Photocopying permitted by license only

Ballerinos en Pointe: Les Ballets Trockadero de Monte Carlo

Bud Coleman

Les Ballets Trockadero de Monte Carlo was founded in 1974 by a small group of performers for the purpose of presenting a playful, entertaining view of traditional, classical ballet in parody form and *en travesti*. The Trocks have performed in 41 states and in Washington, D.C., and internationally in over a hundred cities in thirteen countries. Not only is the Trockadero the only comedic dance company which has been financially successful, it is the oldest all-male dance ensemble in America.

For twenty years the Trocks have presented a very complicated performance matrix which includes simultaneous and often conflicting gender codes. By exploring the range of these presentations, how interpretations of these presentations have changed over time and how they often shift according to where they are performed, the Trocks become a point of inquiry into gender and gender illusion.

KEY WORDS   Les Ballets Trockadero de Monte Carlo, travesty, comic dance, parody, dance history.

Les Ballets Trockadero de Monte Carlo was founded in 1974 by a small group of performers for the purpose of presenting a playful, entertaining view of traditional, classical ballet and modern dance in parody form and *en travesti*. From their start, presenting midnight performances in Greenwich Village lofts, the Trocks inspired glowing reviews from major publications like *The New Yorker*, *Vogue*, *Time*, *Newsweek*, and *People*, leading the company to larger Off-Off-Broadway theaters. In 1976 the company performed in Canada, at the Brooklyn Academy of Music, signed with Sheldon Soffer Management, and qualified for the National Endowment for the Arts Dance Touring Program. One year later, the Trockadero appeared on national television in a Shirley MacLaine special, and on Broadway at the Palace Theatre. In the last twenty years, the

Trocks have performed in 41 states and in Washington, D.C., in addition to international tours which have taken them to over a hundred cities in twelve countries on six continents. In a pilgrimage to their spiritual homeland (the land of Petipa), the Trocks made their Russian debut in 1994, presenting 14 performances in Moscow, St. Petersburg, Lithuania, and Siberia. Not only is the Trockadero the only comedic dance company in the world which has been financially successful, it is the longest running all-male dance ensemble in America. Ted Shawn's Men Dancers performed for seven years, from 1933 to 1940.

The original concept of Les Ballets Trockadero de Monte Carlo has not changed since its inception. It is a company of professional male dancers performing a full range of contemporary dance and classical ballet repertoire, investing them with a wicked sense of humor throughout the entire proceedings. Over the years, the technical proficiency of the dancers has improved to match their comic expertise. Several Trocks who specialize in female roles can execute thirty-two *fouettés en pointe*, a virtuosic sequence traditionally performed in *Black Swan pas de deux* and *Don Quixote pas de deux*.

A Trock performance can be analyzed from at least five points of reference: (1) the quality of the choreography (as original work, as a burlesque of a part of the canon, as a parody of an established style); (2) the technical skill of the dancers; (3) the entertainment/humor quotient; (4) the production values of decor and costuming, etc.; and (5) the gender constructs presented on stage. These categories are by no means autonomous components of a performance, however. Rather, they overlap, intersect, and exist in such a confluent flux that it would serve little purpose to investigate each item independently. Since the company's identity (and marketing strategy) is focused on its composition, that it is an all-male company which performs *en travesti*, the issue of gender (re)presentation becomes the most telling "lens" through which to view the company.

Centuries of social pressure have frozen men and women into very strict and limited physical vocabularies. There is a seemingly finite stock of signifiers of what is considered masculine or feminine because the official colors are black and white, male and female. Intermediate shades do not receive the Good Housekeeping Seal of Approval. The sissy, the tomboy, and other gender benders inspire a (generally derogatory) label because they fall outside of the binary coding system. While the theater is often a mirror held up to nature, it can also be a site to posit alternate "realities." When posture, gesture, and/or behavior is put on stage, it takes on an

Figure 1   Les Ballets Trockadero de Monte Carlo. Four Little Swans in *Swan Lake*, Act II. From Left to Right: Clinton W. Smith, Brent Mason, Joel Paley, and Leland Walsh. Photo: Kenn Duncan.

iconic value, heightening and drawing attention to cultural designations. How these staged signs of gender are to be interpreted may or may not follow the author's intent, just as their transmission may or may not employ a sexual body identical to the gender body (re)presented. The stage presentation may purposely mix male and female codes, resisting traditional binary gender coding; the resultant image is neither black nor white, but rather, zebra striped. A Trockadero performance finds a comfortable parallel in the 1994 film, *The Adventures of Priscilla—Queen of the Desert*. Remember the bloke who traveled to the Australian outback with a dream? "To be a cock in a frock on a rock." In the case of the Trockadero ballerino, he is a weenie in a Niccolini acting like a queenie.

The Trocks' official stand is that they are not impersonating women, but impersonating ballerinas. While most would suggest that the person of ballerina is inextricably linked to the cultural construct of woman, the argument is basically semantic since the gender matrix of ballerina and woman overlaps under the heading of feminine. The intent of the Trock presentation is not meant to fool the audience into thinking they are watching women on stage. There is no "reveal" at the end of a Trock performance; the dancers do not doff their wigs to surprise the audience with the fact that they are genetic males. There is little need for this gimmick since mixed gender constructs are an integral part of the performance. While the Trock dancer appearing as Odette in Act II of *Swan Lake* dons the pink pointe shoes and tights, the pancake tutu, and the requisite array of white feathers; he also paints on the caricature of a ballerina face, does not shave his chest or arm pits, utilizes no bust pads to approximate a bosom, and can do little to hide the silhouette of his male frame. While on stage, the Trock ballerina may comment on the character he is portraying in a particular ballet, but the dancer never breaks character in order to comment on himself as a ballerina.

The majority of the ballets the Trockadero perform are the traditional "work horses" in the classical ballet repertory: *Swan Lake* Act II, *Giselle* Act II, *Les Sylphides*, *Pas de Quatre*. Humor arises in *how* the choreography is being performed and *who* is performing it, not because the choreography is inherently comic. Even though little in classical ballet choreography is humorous, what is advantageous to the Trockadero is that the plots of most story ballets are decidedly silly. While the Ivanov/Petipa choreography for *Swan Lake* is universally acclaimed for its sublime beauty, the plot of the story is basically

Figure 2 Les Ballets Trockadero de Monte Carlo. (Sanson Candelaria) Alexis Lermontov and (Natch Taylor) Tamara Boumdiyeva in *Swan Lake*. Photo: John L Murphy.

ludicrous. A prince, wandering about in the woods, falls in love with a big white bird. Even though he has sworn to be true to her, he later falls in love with a big black bird, and this last event he does in front of his own mother at a party!

Regardless of the less-than-probable stories of most 19th century ballets, the Trocks derive humor from them not by commenting on the plots, but rather by concentrating on *how* the choreography is performed. It is worth noting that dance steps have no gender, it is the execution of steps that project gender. As founding co-director of the Trocks Peter Anastos told Hilary Ostlere, "Pointe work has no gender. It's not the exclusive property of women. It hurts *every-body*" (Ostlere, 1976, p. 15). The Trock preparation for a step might be exaggerated, or the movement may begin with the wrong point of initiation, or a muscled preparation may lead up to nothing more than a single *pirouette*. The possibilities for physical humor are end-less. Keith Glancy's Natalia Zlotmachinskaya made a career out of being a sort of Edward Gorey ballerina, the one with osteoporosis. William Zamora's Zamarina Zamarkova's Marie Taglioni was so arthritic you could swear you heard her joints creak as he moved.

What is equally important in the Trock performance is not only *how* the choreography is performed, but *who* is performing the chore-ography. At 200 pounds, Richard Goldberger's Olga Plushinskaya literally defied the laws of gravity when he got up *en pointe*. And there was no getting around the fact that Peter Anastos' Olga Tchikaboumskaya was extremely hairy. Large tufts of body hair is not the image that immediately comes to mind when one dreams of the ideal sylph, swan, or wili.

Arlene Croce, dance critic for *The New Yorker*, wrote about the company in the first month of their existence, September, 1974. Her early reviews not only gave the fledging company much needed publicity, but, more importantly, gave them a credibility that was not implicit in their midnight performances in a homophile center on 14th street. Croce explained the basis of humor in the company's work as simply the effort of something heavy trying to be light. She wrote that "Drag ballet provides one answer to the question of why men impersonating women are funny, while women impersonating men are not; it has to do with gravity. (A heavy thing trying to become light is automatically funnier than a light thing trying to become heavy)" (Croce, 1979, p. 80). Other critics have suggested that the humor in a Trock performance is more related to gender than it is to physical weight or bulk. By adopting female-coded clothing and gestures, men are laughable because they are relinquishing the superiority of their birthright, whereas when women cross the gender line in male-coded clothing and gestures, this act is seen as subversive and potentially dangerous.

In her analysis of gender issues present in a Trock performance, Croce turned to the French poet and philosopher Stéphane Mallarmé. Mallarmé suggests that a ballerina is not a woman dancing, because she isn't a woman and she doesn't dance. Dance, in Mallarmé's view, is "preeminently the theatrical form of poetry," and therefore the ballerina is a metaphor. She is one who writes poems with her body, who appears before us as a vessel teeming with abstract preliterate suggestions. Forever a symbol, the ballerina is never a person (Croce, 1979, p. 76).

Through the years, the Trockadero's official "company statement" to interviewers has followed this Mallarmé/Croce model: they are impersonating ballerinas, not women. Besides aligning themselves with high art, this rhetoric attempts to steer the Trocks away from the gender issue. For seventeen years as artistic director of the Trockadero, Natch Taylor remained true to this position. This 1989 interview with Barbara Newman (*Dancing Times*) is typical of Taylor's elaborate two-stepping around the gender issue.

The thing is, we're not making a comment about men doing women's roles, we're not making a comment on drag, as it were. We're just making a comment on ballet and having fun with ballet.... But there's nothing sexual about our dancing or about being male or female or anything else. (Newman, 1989, p. 345)

Taylor contends that "A ballerina isn't a woman, she's a choreographic machine" (Temin, 1981, p. A20). Over the last twenty years, the Trocks have hired few true transvestites, men who cross dress regularly as an integral facet of their gender identity off the stage. Taylor remarked: "they don't last. We're not what they want. They want to make it as real as possible. The company isn't a vent for fantasies because we work too hard. We aren't female impersonators at all. That isn't our intent; we're not out to fool the public" (Pappas, 1981, p. G4).

Intent is one thing; perception is something else. Regardless of how many press releases the Trocks have issued since 1974, repeating over and over that they are not drag queens, each audience member is free to "read" this event as they wish. Though it can be informative to look at a Trock performance through the spectacles of their official intent, we are by no means restricted to this perspective.

While Jill Dolan has never written about Les Ballets Trockadero de Monte Carlo specifically, she has done a great deal of groundbreaking work concerning gender constructs in performance. Dolan contends that men, heterosexual or homosexual, do not have as much at stake in the gender arena since they historically control theater, the mirror that reflects society. Dolan aligns gender illusionists closer to straight men than to homosexual communities, since men in drag can easily don the clothes of the cultural elite when they are off the stage. She dismisses most gay male drag from the field of serious gender investigation since it is generally a product of camp. Here, Dolan relies on Susan Sontag's treatise on camp. For Sontag, camp sensibility emphasizes style over content, has a love of artifice, and is purposefully disengaged from underlying meaning. In light of recent repositionings of the term, camp as a political, queer, cultural critique, Sontag's definition of camp, first published in 1964, is quaintly (or annoyingly) old-fashioned. While there is no one standard definition of camp, new or old, in general it delights in artificiality, exaggeration, and affectation, especially when used in conjunction with banality, irony, and/or kitsch. Yet, even embracing Sontag's tenet of camp, in which style is emphasized over content, does not necessitate that the content that is present should not be analyzed. Dismissing gender illusion because the author of this gender disarray is male is ignoring a rich arena of analysis. Dolan does so, however, because she believes that when the drag queen is on stage, woman is invisible.

Until 1660, when women were legally permitted to act in London theaters, woman's stage image in most of Western drama was completely controlled by men. Men wrote the words that came out of other men's mouths, men who were literally acting for women. It is incorrect, however, to apply the same model of gender studies to the entire span of performance history. From the classical Greeks to the Renaissance, women were never seen nor heard on stage. This differs from the last 400 years in which women have, even in a limited sense, been able to perform and write for the stage. Since 1660, when one sex appropriates gender codes traditionally associated with the opposite sex, the absent sex is there, often powerfully so, because of its absence. In the case of the Trockadero performance, the reality of a powerful absence not only applies to the person of woman, it also applies to the archetypal perfection of dance. In a Trock performance, in which comic dance is presented *en travesti*, what is presented is just as important as what is missing: women

Figure 3 Les Ballets Trockadero de Monte Carlo. Olga Plushinskaya (Richard Goldberger) in *The Dance of Liberation of the American People in Homage to Isadora Duncan, the greatest American Patriot since Betsy Ross, Barbara Fritchie, and Sacagawea.* Photo: John L Murphy.

on stage, supple stretched arches, flexible spinal columns, knees that straighten completely, etc.

A great deal of the humor of a Trock performance comes from "breaking the rules," disrupting the propriety of classical ballet and the seriousness of modern dance. Humor can also come about by providing audiences a new perspective on a familiar subject: the silly plot of *Swan Lake*; the histrionics of Graham; and the revelation that gender is a culturally constructed formula that has nothing to do with genital equipment. The same Trock performance can also elicit from audience members copious amounts of laughter for entirely different reasons. From another vantage point, a Trock performance is funny not because it challenges gender coding, but because it reinforces the status quo. In the paradigm of sex-equals-gender, the homosexual is the one who attempts to become the opposite sex via dress and behavior: all lesbians are butch and all gay men are effeminate. From the homophobe's point of view, a Trock performance is humorous because the male dancers look ridiculous in tutus, look awkward executing "feminine" movements, and, well, faggots are funny as long as they are not sexually aggressive: same performance, different reading.

One perspective of a Trock performance that is routinely overlooked by reviewers is the dancers' ability to transcend their male bodies and their level of dance technique to present the presence of a ballerina. Sanson Candelaria (1941–1986) was one such performer. Candelaria combined impeccable comic timing, solid dance technique, and savvy performance skills to create the incomparable Tamara Boumdiyeva. Candelaria transcended the *tendu* and the wig, the eyelashes and the *battement*, to satisfy the reason we go to the theater: to be transported.

Intrinsic to the Trocks' concept of the ballerina is that this creature is larger than life. While cinema performances have influenced acting in the theater, making it more restrained and subtle, the Trocks hearken back to a nineteenth-century acting tradition that embraces flamboyant bravura. Abandoning any sort of "safe" or laid-back performance style, the Trock dancers literally fling themselves into a performance, armed with an outrageousness to match the size of their enormous false eyelashes. This largesse is certainly one of the reasons for the troupe's popularity. By combining the choreography of the ballet stage with madcap antics of the circus, a Trockadero performance is a wonderful antidote to delicate and "refined" high art.

Even in a "regular" dance company, what distinguishes a prima ballerina from a demi-soloist is not only technical proficiency, but also that illusive energy known as presence, that quality that makes the act of executing a simple movement of the arms by one dancer a revelation and by another an inconsequential gesture. Especially during the early years of the Trockadero, its dancers often had little else but presence to offer an audience; they acted like they were ballerinas instead of dancing like ballerinas. As Francis Herridge (*New York Post*) said of Antony Bassae/Tamara Karpova in 1975: "His technique is barely good enough but the assurance he exudes makes you feel 'she' is superb" (Herridge, 1975, n. pag.). Observing Bassae (1943–1985) perform the female role in *Le Corsaire pas de deux*, Robert Talmage of *Dance Magazine* thought it the most entertaining rendition of this classic he had ever seen.

And considering Karpova looks like a cross between a barrel-chested tenor and a frog on two legs, so much more the marvel. Her feet are almost indescribable. The right is short and hooked, but allows her an occasional balance. The left is not so fortunate. Picture Cinderella's sisters actually getting the glass slipper on, and you have a sense of Karpova's left pied. It's all knuckles and joints, hanging over the sides of the shoe and it never, repeat never, points correctly. But be that as it may, she flies about the stage, underslung jaw set bulldog fashion, with a smile to dazzle the gods. She doesn't do all the steps, but I can think of others who don't either. And not worrying about it gives her wonderful freedom. (Talmage, 1976, p. 78)

Indeed, the knowledge that perfection is impossible gives the Trock ballerina an advantage over his female counterpart since the former can devote energy into facets of his performance other than technical proficiency.

Arlene Croce also fell under the spell of Antony Bassae as he appeared as La Karpova, the self-proclaimed "black rhinestone of Russian Ballet." To Croce, Karpova looked like a cross between "a pug version of Lou Costello," and "a bulldog standing on its hind legs." As Kitri in Peter Anastos' *Reader's Digest* staging of *Don Quixote*, Bassae delivered a performance that inspired Croce to proclaim that "Karpova, I believe, gave a better performance than the Bolshoi's Nina Sorokina" who was dancing at the Met at the time. "Though the two performances are not to be compared technically, there was more wit, more plasticity, more elegance, and even more femininity in Karpova's balances and kneeling backbends than in all of Sorokina's tricks, and the way Karpova used her snap-open fan put the Bolshoi to shame" (Croce, 1979, p. 80). This heady announcement from one of New York's leading dance critics, that a male dancer in drag, dancing in a broken-down loft, essayed the role of Kitri more impressively than a member of the Bolshoi was nothing less than stunning. When a Trock is good, it isn't about technique, it isn't about gender, it's about presence.

One curious facet of the Trockadero's checkered past is that while the repertoire has stayed basically the same over the last twenty years, how the company has been "read" has changed significantly. The Trocks' original audience were balletomanes, predominately gay, who knew the ballets and personalities being parodied. Indeed, the first performing venue for the Trockadero was the Westside Discussion Group, a homophile organization on 14th street. But in 1977, the Trocks changed their audience; they were on a Shirley MacLaine television special, and appeared for two weeks at the Palace Theatre on Broadway. When the Trockadero hit the road, Middle America was now their audience. They are folks who have often heard about *Swan Lake* or *Giselle*, but who have never had much opportunity to see classical ballet, and rarely know anything about modern choreographers such as Isadora Duncan, Martha Graham, Paul Taylor, Pina Bausch, who are the other targets of the Trockadero's satiric observation. In addition to a shift in their core audience base, another crucial change affected the "reading" of the Trockadero. From 100 seat Off-Off-Broadway performing spaces, the Trocks were now booked into 1,000, 2,000, and 3,000 seat road houses. The same ten-member company whose dancing filled the tiny postage-stamp sized stages of the Village now looked precariously thin on a large stage.

As drag became more visible in theater, film, and television in the 70s and 80s, the shock value of seeing a man in female-coded gender illusion was no longer so unusual in New York, yet Middle America continued to find the Trocks unique and outrageous. Until the Jesse Helms inspired hysteria concerning "homoerotic" content in publicly funded art, the Trocks enjoyed a very lucrative market on the road, performing only occasionally in New York after 1977. (The Trockadero has never received direct funding from the NEA, but has been booked by many sponsors who do, which is why the Helms amendment to the NEA application directly affected the company. No promoter was going to book the Trockadero and run the risk of losing his or her entire NEA funding by booking an act which might be labeled homoerotic. Overnight, the Trocks' American market virtually disappeared.)

Figure 4   Antony Bassae as Tamara Karpova in *Carmen*.

Not only has time affected the readings of a Trock performance, so has place. South Africa, South America, Australia, Europe, and now, Russia, have all enjoyed performances by the Trocks. But it has been the Japanese who have responded most enthusiastically to the company. In 1996, the Trockadero celebrated its twelfth tour of Japan. These are tours; in addition to Tokyo, the company has appeared in over thirty different Japanese cities. In a different culture, why has the Trocks' depiction of satires of Western dance, and caricatures of ballerinas produced so much laughter? And in Japan, why is it important that the parody be performed by Americans? The Trocks do not have a copyright or trademark on their concept and do not produce themselves, so there is nothing prohibiting their Japanese promoter from creating and/or booking a Japanese "Trockadero" in order to save money. This has not occurred because the Japanese promoter knows his audiences like Les Ballets Trockadero de Monte Carlo just the way they are. While there are centuries-old Japanese performing traditions of gender illusion (Noh, Kabuki, Takarazuka), these forms do not derive humor from the convention of travesty. I suggest that for the Japanese, the cultural distinction of who (nationality) is performing the gender illusion is just as important as what sex they are (male).

The Trocks have defied common sense, business acumen, bunions, Jesse Helms, and tour-schedules-from-hell to entertain legions of fans around the world. Few enterprises that literally start off as a joke among friends ever achieve the level of notoriety, artistry, and sheer magic that have been, and are, the Trocks. Enthusiastically embracing the rhinestone-and-banana-peel aesthetic, the troupe continues to bedevil those who try to pin it down.

References

Croce, A. (1979) The Two Trockaderos. Rev. of Les Ballets Trockadero de Monte Carlo and Trockadero Gloxinia Ballet Company. In *Afterimages*. New York: Vintage Books.

Dolan, J. (1992) Gender Impersonation Onstage: Destroying or Maintaining the Mirror of Gender Codes. In *Gender in Performance*. Ed. Laurence Senelick. Hanover, New Hampshire: University Press of New England.

Herridge, F. (1975, March 28) Ballet Laffs. Rev. of Les Ballets Trockadero de Monte Carlo. *New York Post*, n. pag.

Newman, B. (1989, January) Natch Taylor. *Dancing Times*, 342–345.

Ostlere, H. (1976, December 2) Putting On By Sending Up. *East Side Express* [New York City], 15.

Pappas, N. (1981, March 15) Trocks' Travesty is Not a Drag. *The Hartford Courant*, G1, G4.

Sontag, S. (1983) *A Susan Sontag Reader*. New York: Vintage Books.

Talmage, R. (1976, March) Perspectives: New York. Rev. of Les Ballets Trockadero de Monte Carlo. *Dance Magazine*, 76–78.

Temin, C. (1981, November 22) Men in tutus and tiaras. *Boston Globe*, A11, A20.

Choreography and Dance
1998, Vol. 5, Part 1, pp. 25–37
Photocopying permitted by license only

© 1998 OPA (Overseas Publishers Association) N.V.
Published by license under
the Harwood Academic Publishers imprint,
part of The Gordon and Breach Publishing Group.
Printed in India.

Life Dances: Jawole Willa Jo Zollar's Choreographic Construction of Black Womanhood

Veta Goler

African American women have a legacy of invisibility. Historically, they were ostensibly included within the categories of "women" or "blacks;" however, such references often translated as *white* women or black *men*. Black women remained invisible and oppressed by race and gender, and frequently, by class.

Autobiography is a weapon in African American women's fight against oppression. By defining and constructing themselves in writing, they achieve visibility and claim their own self-worth. Choreography is Jawole Willa Jo Zollar's weapon.

This paper examines Zollar's construction and affirmation of black womanhood. Her thematic choices, the ways she subverts stereotypic images of black women, her presentation of black women within community contexts, and her foregrounding of race and gender all parallel black women's written autobiographical work. Discussion of Zollar's choreography explicates her unique artistry, especially as a form of discourse *on* black women *by* black women and a means of self-affirmation.

KEY WORDS   African American choreographers, autobiography, "Belongso", stereotypic images, Urban Bush Women LifeDance series.

Modern dance has historically been a forum for self-expression and self-affirmation. While the first American modern dance choreographers explored social and political dynamics and cultures of various ethnic groups of American society, in recent years, many choreographers have focused on intimate self-expression. African American choreographers have often made social and political commentary on various aspects of American society and have celebrated black life, creating what singer/composer/scholar Bernice Johnson Reagon calls culturally autobiographical work, in which the expressions of the community are inseparable from the expressions of the self (Friedman, 1988, p. 43). Significantly, the most well-known choreographers creating work referencing black culture in the last few decades have been men, such as Alvin Ailey, Donald McKayle, Rod Rodgers, Eleo Pomare, Garth Fagan, and Bill T. Jones. Jawole Willa Jo Zollar is a contemporary black woman choreographer who provides opportunities for African Americans to look again at their history and culture, from an African American woman's perspective. She creates personally and culturally autobiographical work, drawing on her own life, the lives of her family, friends and ancestors, and on her cultural heritage to create work that affirms black womanhood.

Throughout much of the history of this country, black women have been relegated to positions of low status in American society. Economically, politically, and socially African American women have been among the most disempowered citizens. Their subordinate status is attributable to two significant phenomena of perception. Often, black women have been overlooked, ignored, and invisible members of society. They have also been objectified in stereotypic images which have caused them to be perceived in negative, damaging ways. Both the lack of perception and negative perception have had profound consequences for the black woman's place in society and for her own self-image.

Stereotypic images of African American women originated in slavery to keep them powerless and to justify their mistreatment. This continued to evolve in order to maintain a white supremacist, patriarchal societal order. The oversexed and immoral Jezebel, the maternal, religious, and completely asexual Mammy, Exotic Mulatto, attractive but doomed, the assertive, independent, and defeminized black Matriarch, and Sapphire, the castrating bitch, have been, at different points throughout the African presence in America, the predominant images of black women in historical texts and popular culture.

The resultant impact of these negative images is the perception of African American women as hypersexed, masculinized females whose inherently evil nature allows them only limited capacity for contributing positively to society. These negative stereotypes have historically justified white male sexual abuse of black women, perpetuated the Southern aristocratic way of life and allowed white women to hold superior social positions by virtue of their so-called chastity and domesticity. As a result, much of the blame for the black man's powerlessness and the disruption of the African American family has been placed squarely on the shoulders of the

Figure 5 Jawole Willa Jo Zollar in her *Bitter Tongue*. Photo: Cylla Von Tiedemann.

black woman. The African American woman has suffered from the internalization of the attitudes associated with these stereotypic images and has experienced pervasive self-doubt, self-hatred and low self-esteem.

This devaluation and self-deprecation of black women under-score the need for African American women's autobiography. Through autobiography, black women challenge these detrimental stereotypes by reconstructing their lives through self-discovery and self-creation. As Robert Sayre writes in Albert Stone's *The American Autobiography*:

> A necessary step in anyone's liberation from stereotypes and injustice is the moment when he or she asserts his or her own rights and values against those imposed from without. This is the discovery of self, and it is what has made autobiography such an important ideological weapon. (1981, p. 12)

Autobiography is a resource for the black woman's self-analysis (Blackburn, 1980, p. 147) and encourages her self-healing. Through the autobiographical process she examines and reflects on her experiences from her own perspective. Free from the negative assessments and characterizations of others, the black woman then views her experiences and actions with acceptance and affirmation.

Autobiography

The self is not a static, fixed entity that is traced from life onto the written page. It is actually created as authors write about their lives. Individuals' perceptions of self determine how they approach the autobiographical act.

Men tend to understand themselves as individual and separate from others. They acquire their sense of identity from their work and other activities outside of the home. Men also tend to approach thinking and knowledge with a linear, analytic logic. Consequently, according to Estelle Jelinek in *Women's Autobiography*, the male autobiographer constructs a self that is professional and intellectual through a chronological, linear narrative (Jelinek, 1980, p. 7). This encompasses the individual's work in society and largely omits his family and personal life (1980, p. 7).

In contrast, a woman's sense of identity is much more connected to the community because it develops from her relationships with those around her (Mason, 1980, p. 210). Consequently, her inter-actions and relationships with others are important inclusions in her autobiography making the content of her autobiography, in general, more personal than that of a man's. Women's auto-biographical structure is consistent with their embracing of a vari-ety of modes of understanding: emotional, logical and intuitive. Rather than utilizing a strictly linear or chronological narrative of their life events and experiences, female autobiographers break up the flow of their work, and employ a fragmented, interrupted structure.

For African Americans of both genders, the overarching value of autobiography is in fighting oppression through the self-determi-nation that accompanies self-definition. The ability to name and describe one's experiences, feelings and characteristics, from one's own perspective, is closely linked to an individual's sense of agency. Too often non-black historians and chroniclers of culture have inaccurately and negatively defined black people. African American autobiographers therefore provide information where it is lacking, correct misinformation, document their actions against racist oppression, and communicate survival strategies to others. The legacy of communal social patterns in pre-colonial Africa, and the necessity of collective action during and after slavery in the New World, make the community an important part of black American life and an important aspect of black autobiographical self-construction. African American autobiography is further distin-guished by a number of common themes, among the most preva-lent, family, religion, education, work, interactions with whites, and freedom (physical, mental, and spiritual).

The characteristics of African American women's autobiography relate it to and distinguish it from androcentric and white women's models. The autobiographical works of black women are written with the same fragmented structure as those of white women. They reveal a collective voice which is also evident with white women and black men. And certain themes that characterize the auto-biographies of black men are also found in black women's auto-biographies; however, several dualities both define African American women's identities and reveal the distinctiveness of black female autobiography. Regina Blackburn, in her essay "In Search of the Black Female Self," states that autobiographical work affirms the African American female self in a way that embraces both race and gender, privileges her public and private lives, and

Figure 6   Urban Bush Women. Left to Right Dafinah Blacksher, Jawole Willa Jo Zollar, (seated) Carolina Garcia, Christine King, Michelle Dorant, Kristin McDonald, (kneeling) Dionne Kamara, Amara Tabor-Smith. Photo: Bette Marshall.

connects the autobiographer to her community (Blackburn, 1980, p. 148). Such dualities of black women's affirmation also reveal themselves in the choreography of Jawole Willa Jo Zollar.

Director of the New York City-based company, Urban Bush Women, Zollar locates her work in African and African American folk and religious traditions. Cultural forms which originated in African societies and were reformulated in New World diasporan societies are the fundamental materials with which she builds her dances. Zollar presents these cultural explorations through the prism of her womanist/radical feminist viewpoint and addresses social and political issues common to old and new cultures. By privileging race and gender, the primary components of black women's identities, Zollar builds dances that illuminate and construct these identities.

In African American women's autobiographies, issues of race may include an author's sense of identity, her experiences with color dynamics in the black community, and instances of racism. Similarly, while some black women write about sexist oppression in their autobiographies, others make little direct reference to sexism. Instead, they express the implications of the author's femaleness solely in terms of identity and sexuality.

In Zollar's choreography, race reveals itself both in her distinctive artistry and her subject matter. She bases much of her movement vocabulary on esteemed scholar/choreographer Katherine Dunham's Afro-Caribbean technique. Zollar accompanies her works with African-based percussion, jazz music, and her dancers' harmonic and rhythmic vocalizations founded in slave field hollers and calls. The interdisciplinary aspect of her work has precedents in West African worship and performance traditions. In addition, Zollar's explorations of black folk culture and worship are thematically African-based. Race is so fundamental to her dance that she no longer accepts white dancers in her company and admits only black dancers with strong African American cultural experiences (Zollar, 1992).

The body is perhaps the most important factor of a person's sense of self, especially as it relates to gender and sexuality; however, beauty standards are culturally determined. Consequently, black women's physicality is a race issue, an issue which Zollar celebrates and affirms. The beauty of black women is evident as soon as her company takes the stage; Urban Bush Women is a stunning mosaic of black womanhood. Each dancer is distinctly different from the

Figure 7   Urban Bush Women in Jawole Willa Jo Zollar's *Lipstick. A Doo-Wop Dilemma*. Left to Right: Terri Cousar, Treva Offutt, Christine King, Beverley Prentice-Ryan, Maia Claire Garrison, Valerie Winborne. Photo: Cylla Von Tiedemann.

others. The different shades of brown of the dancers' skin tones are part of the variety in African American coloration. Their different body types, ranging from tall and thin to short and stocky, reflect Zollar's expansive sense of black women's beauty and the African aesthetic which values women's large hips and thighs as well. In fact, in her piece, *A Dance...Batty Moves*, for which a program note indicates that "batty" is Jamaican slang for "the butt," the movement and form-revealing costume accentuate this culturally important part of black women's bodies.

Zollar celebrates the culture of black women as she privileges gender through the personnel in her company, the company's name, and much of her choreography. In addition to relatively light-hearted works expressing aspects of black femaleness such as friendship in *Girlfriends*, drill teams and college step shows in *I Don't Know but I've Been Told, If You Keep on Dancin' You'll Never Grow Old*, and anatomy in *A Dance...Batty Moves*, Zollar creates pieces that make political commentary on such issues as societal devaluation of women and sexual violence. She incorporates specific experiences from her own life to illustrate these problems. In *Womb Wars*, from her *LifeDance* series (a series of spiritually auto-biographical solos), Zollar points out that in a number of cultures, people respond to the birth of a "womb child," (a girl child) with the words, "Oh shit!" Her mother uttered these same words when Zollar was born. In contrast, when Zollar gave birth to her own daughter, she greeted her with "Thank God!" Within the work Zollar makes less explicit reference to other events in her life. She talks about incest and rape, indicating that at age ten she learned through a "trusted family friend, who wasn't really a trusted family friend," about the relationship between the threat of violence and sexual submission.

Another dance, *Lipstick*, begins as an adolescent exploration and declaration of budding sexuality and womanhood. Each dancer declares "lipstick is my weapon" and assumes a sultry, seductive pose from one of the fashion magazines. The talk progresses to boyfriends named Rubio and then to Uncle Rubio who chases Auntie Roman around the house at gunpoint. When the domestic dispute has ended, apparently without bloodshed, Uncle Rubio comforts his niece, the narrator. She describes him taking her upstairs and cleaning her legs of the urine she released in her terror, and makes a veiled reference to incest, flatly repeating a statement she has made several times earlier in the dance, "Jimmy Baldwin 'tween my legs."

Zollar not only presents such painful aspects of African American women's experiences, she encourages their self-healing. Zollar begins her *LifeDance* solo, *The Papess*, dressed in a long blue raincoat, wearing high heels and long gloves. Her long dreadlocked hair is wrapped and held on top of her head with a scarf. Facing upstage, she moves sensuously, at some points with the seemingly innocent glamour of a beauty contestant, and at others with the overt sexuality of a woman who earns her living by renting her body. When she turns to face front, however, she pulls a knife from a pocket and brandishes it about. She is a tough, hardened woman. Near the end of the piece Zollar removes her raincoat, and wearing only a beaded belt, takes the scarf from her hair, wraps it around her waist and hips, and drapes it over a shoulder. Kneeling on the floor, she smashes an egg on her chest and rubs it over her arms and bare breasts. To Zollar, the character's hardness stems from her devastating experiences of incest and sexual abuse (Zollar, 1993). The ritualized actions of smearing the egg are symbolic of her efforts to reclaim her erotic nature, of re-valuing her sexuality, an important part of her recovery process (Zollar, 1993).

While race and gender are the major aspects of their identity, class is an issue for both self-definition and self-determination for many black women. In *Womb Wars*, Zollar critiques the erosion of women's power over their own bodies. She counsels her friend Marsha, who is "in crisis," asking her what she will do since "they're taking away our rights." It is harder to find doctors who will perform "the procedure." Reproductive rights are an important class issue for many lower-class black women who have limited access to medical practitioners who can assist with either the continuation or termination of pregnancies.

One of Zollar's clearest commentaries on class is *Shelter*, her powerful denunciation of homelessness. African drumming and text about the distance of African Americans from the Motherland evoke images of comfort at returning home. The dancers are visibly distressed, however. They are chased and thrown around the stage by some unseen force, moving back and forth like weary nomads trying to find a place to sleep. In one version, there is a point when they all lie on their sides shivering, an exquisitely moving moment as the dancers' vibrating intensifies. They shiver so intensely that they roll onto their backs and their legs and arms stick up in the air like dead animals. At the same time, Zollar reads Laurie Carlos's impassioned text, "Belongso," about saving black children from

Figure 8 Urban Bush Women in Jawole Willa Jo Zollar's *Shelter*. (Left to Right: Treva Offutt, Beverley Prentice-Ryan, Maia Claire Garrison, Christine King, Valerie Winborne, Terri Cousar). Photo: Cylla Von Tiedemann.

extinction and the earth from destruction. Without the Earth, we are all homeless.

For black women, self-identity is constructed in relationship to the black female community. Through their heritage of black cultural experiences and legacy of oppression by and resistance to racism and sexism, black women understand themselves relative to other black women. Historically, from the female networks in the family compounds of traditional African societies to the club movement and extended families of the New World, black women have supported and affirmed each other. Both Zollar's choreography and the very existence of her company recognize this tradition, speak to her own affirmation of black women, and provide a medium through which their voices can be heard.

In addition to its dualities of race and gender and self and community, the black woman-self is also characterized by a duality of personal and public existences. Most African American women autobiographers reveal much about their private lives. Since most black women work outside of their homes, however, their public lives are also important and work is typically a significant inclusion in black female autobiographies. Zollar's public performance of intimate details from her own life and from the lives of other black women embodies this public/private duality.

Through her expressions of race and gender in her choreography, her presentation of private experiences in public forums, and her celebration of black women as individuals and in community with others, Zollar reveals much about black women's identities. The realistic and multidimensional images of black women in her work, like black women's written autobiography, encourage self-definition.

In an article about Urban Bush Women, art historian Lowery Stokes Sims documents thoughts of Laurie Carlos, a writer, actor, and frequent collaborator of Zollar's, which concern limitations in theatrical roles for African American women.

Carlos explicates her dissatisfaction with the female characters that are usually delineated for black women in theater—either asexual (and fat) virgin mother, or whore. As Carlos noted she wanted to play the role of a whore who was "a mother, a grandmother and a good cook." These were the women that she knew. (Sims, 1989, p. 27)

Like Carlos, Zollar seeks to present realistic images of black women that counter outdated or culturally inappropriate conceptions of womanhood. For example, Zollar was criticized for her "stereo-typic" presentation of the Granny character in *Praise House*. She agrees that Carlos, who plays Granny and is short and round, fits certain grandmotherly imagery but asserts that Granny seems stereotypic because she is realistic. Zollar asks, What does your grandmother look like? To avoid presenting Granny as a unidimensional, and therefore truly stereotypic character, she reveals Granny's complexity through her matronly, and seemingly asexual shape, the ribald recipe for cobbler she sings in order to enter heaven, the visions which enable her to paint and which cause others to question her sanity, her gentle and affectionate love for her grand-daughter, and her deep spirituality.

In presenting dances which privilege race and gender and address issues of class, Zollar, like black women autobiographical writers, empowers herself and others like her by enacting self-construction. Through her work, black women see their experiences articulated and validated. They see others who look like them presented as complex individuals and, thus, their own identities are affirmed. Such affirmation of self is an important function of autobiographical endeavors and makes Zollar's dance an important tool for black women's self-liberation.

References

Blackburn, R. (1980) In search of the black female self; African-American women's autobiographies and ethnicity. In E.C. Jelinek (Ed.), *Women's Autobiography: Essays in Criticism* (pp. 133–148). Bloomington: Indiana University Press.

Friedman, S.S. (1988) Women's autobiographical selves: Theory and practice. In S. Benstock (Ed.), *The Private Self: Theory and Practice of Women's Autobiographical Writings* (pp. 34–62). Chapel Hill: University of North Carolina Press.

Jelinek, E.C. (1980) Women's autobiography and the male tradition. Chapter in *Women's Autobiography: Essays in Criticism*. Bloomington: Indiana University Press.

Mason, M.G. (1980) The other voice: Autobiographies of women writers. In J. Olney (Ed.), *Autobiography: Essays Theoretical and Critical* (pp. 207–235). Princeton, NJ: Princeton University Press.

Sayre, R.E. (1981) The proper study: Autobiographies in American studies. In A. Stone (Ed.), *The American Autobiography: A Collection of Critical Essays* (pp. 11–30). Englewood Cliffs, NJ: Prentice-Hall.

Sims, L.S. (Spring, 1989) 'Heat' and other climatic manifestations: Urban Bush Women, Thought Music and Craig Harris and the Dirty Tones Band. *High Performance* no. 45, 22–27.

Zollar, J.W.J. (1992) Interview by author, 2 April, Atlanta, GA. Tape recording.

———. (1993) Interview by author, 29 October, New York City. Tape recording.

Choreography and Dance
1998, Vol. 5, Part 1, pp. 39–51
Photocopying permitted by license only

Techno Bodies or, Muscling with Gender in Contemporary Dance

Ann Cooper Albright

The one overwhelming image I have of La La La Human Steps' multi-media extravaganza *Infante, C'est Destroy* is of Louise Lecavalier flying through the air like a human torpedo. My essay uses the example of Lecavalier's dancing in order to bring to the foreground the complexities of talking about the physical body and gender in contemporary dance. Thinking about Lecavalier's body, its delineated muscles and fierce physicality, as well as its position within Lock's spectacle, brings us right up against one of the most ferociously contested issues in feminist and cultural studies today. What is the status of the female body as biologically determined or culturally constructed? In what ways can a woman physically break out of the traditional representation of the "feminine" body in dance, and in what ways does the "feminine" become literally re-incorporated to accomodate the changing fashions of physical being?

KEY WORDS   Gender, contemporary dance, women, muscle, feminism, Louise Lecavalier.

The one overwhelming image I have of La La La Human Steps' multi-media extravaganza *Infante, C'est Destroy* is of Louise Lecavalier flying through the air like a human torpedo. She gets caught by another dancer, thrashes around with him for a while, then vaults right out of his arms and halfway across the stage, only to rebound back into his face. A few minutes and who knows how many heartbeats later, she rears up from the floor one last time, shakes her mane of bleached-blond hair and struts off the stage with an attitude that would make the most vicious heavy metal rocker look like Pete Seeger by comparison.

Louise Lecavalier is the star of Édouard Lock's dance 'n rock creation which I witnessed during the 1993 Festival International de Nouvelle Danse in Montreal. Throughout this non-stop, 75 minute spectacle, Lecavalier's body, both its hardened aerobic energy and its filmed image, is continuously on display. Pitted against the pounding sounds of Skinny Puppy, Janitors Animated, David Van Tiegham and Einsturzende Neubauten, her dancing uses the driving beat of the music to stretch dance movements to the outer limits of physical possibility and endurance. At one point, Lecavalier grabs one of the various mikes littered around the stage and, panting, begins to discuss the metaphysical dimensions of music, heartbeats, and physical energy. She then produces a mini-mike which she solemnly attaches to percussionist Jackie Gallant's chest. With the kind of cosmic, synergistic intensity which makes heavy metal so seductive to teenagers, Gallant begins to pound away at her drum. The harder Gallant drums, the faster her heartbeat. The faster her heartbeat, the faster she drums to keep up. As Gallant builds quickly to the orgasmic peak of her auto-aerobic union with the drum, Lecavalier comes crashing back to center stage, riding the musical tidal wave just as Gallant finishes.

The first ten minutes of Lecavalier's dancing are absolutely awe-inspiring. Within a few minutes, her well-defined muscles are pumped up and her body is practically pulsating with untapped energy. The way she launches her body across the floor and at various partners is phenomenal. Physically, she is immensely powerful, a fact noted by audience members and dance reviewers alike. Lecavalier is repeatedly described in the lobby, as well as in the press, as a "human torpedo," a "canonball," a "rocket," or a "bullet." Similarly, her physique is ubiquitously evoked through the popular language of body building as either "chiselled," "ripped," or "granite." One reviewer even took these pervasive images of violence to their logical extreme, comparing the dancing of La La La Human Steps to a war. "Arms swing menancingly like knives, legs flash like bayonets, hips are thrust forward with the aggressiveness and rapidity of machine gunfire, and whole bodies fly like rockets through the air."[1]

I find the obsessiveness with which reviewers discuss Lecavalier's body and movement, and the inevitable violent or machine-like metaphors, indicative of a certain unease with Lecavalier's corporeality. Her all encompassing focus on vaulting back and forth across the stage creates an intense physicality that both literally and figuratively *crosses over* gender norms, even in the midst of a cultural moment in which both men and women are encouraged to cultivate a muscularly defined look in their bodies. By taking on the musculature and powerful, explosive movement that marks the achievement of high masculinity in sports, martial arts, and Arnold Schwartzenneger movies, Lecavalier's dancing personna is not easily contained in the role of "prima ballerina," even though Lock's choreography is so obviously an elaborate vehicle for the display of her extraordinary physicality. After the first ten minutes of the spectacle, however, Lecavalier's dancing begins to feel increasingly coerced. Whether she is framed by the camera as in the huge, blown up films of her falling slowly through space, or by the men onstage, Lecavalier never seems to be able to break out of Lock's own vision of her body.

Édouard Lock is a film-maker, a photographer, and a director of mega pop spectacles. Critics frequently call Lecavalier his muse, likening her role in *Infante, C'est Destroy* to a blend of Madonna and Joan of Arc. Visually they have a point. In the filmed section of the dance, she is dressed in metal armor. While she is performing live onstage, Lecavalier flaunts the same kind of sexualized power that Madonna has successfully commodified—what I call the black leather tits and ass and biceps, abs, and quads look. But unlike Madonna, Lecavalier doesn't immediately relieve the cultural anxiety produced by her cross-dressing with a reassuringly feminine voice. Neither, however, does she embody spiritual power or usurp the male perogative in quite the way that I've always imagined Joan of Arc did. The powerful implications of her physicality are eventually diluted by the relentless repetition of the same old stunts. Most of the time, Lecavalier and her two female backups, Pim Boonprakob and Sarah Williams, dance around in various stages of undress, frequently throwing themselves at the male dancers who are usually dressed in suits. In contrast to her male partners, Lecavalier is either totally naked, topless, or dressed in a black bustier and tight see-through shorts. Occasionally she will sport a black leather jacket, but usually that is when she is wearing nothing else on top. My point, of course, is not that the women get naked onstage, it is that they are the *only* ones who do so.

I have introduced this essay with the example of Lecavalier's dancing in order to bring to the foreground the complexities of talking about the physical body and gender in contemporary dance. How, for instance, can we account for the fact that Lecavalier's dancing at once provides the means for, and yet simultaneously resists, the paternalistic gaze of Lock's choreography? In what ways can a woman physically break out of the traditional representation of the "feminine" body, and in what ways does the "feminine" become literally re-incorporated to accomodate the changing fashions of physical being? As Judith Butler quite rightly warns us in her book *Gender Trouble*: "The female body that is freed from the shackles of the paternal law may well prove to be yet another incarnation of that law, posing as subversive but operating in the service of that law's self-amplification and proliferation."[2]

My desire to think carefully through the experience and representation of women's physicality comes from my joint perspective as a dancer and a critic. I began dancing seriously in the early 80s and my preferred movement style is rambunctious and physically challenging. When I see Lecavalier's dancing, I feel the thrill of her movement as my physical imagination translates her motions into my bodily consciousness. I know what it feels like to take some of those flying leaps and I get pleasure from seeing her do it. To a point. My physical consciousness is also attuned to another kind of knowing, that of spending the last ten years reading feminist theory and writing about dance. My initial kinesthetic excitement with Lecavalier's dancing quickly ebbs as I also experience the relentless posturing and physical attack of her movements as well as the sexist frames of Lock's choreography. This is not to suggest that my academic feminist consciousness intellectually inhibits or represses the physical pleasure of seeing her move. Watching dance for me is never either just a physical practice or simply an intellectual process, but rather a full-bodied combination of both. I see not only movement, steps, or aesthetic composition in dance, but also a whole social world onstage. Looking at the ways that world gets constructed in dance allows me to introduce issues of power, gender, sexuality, identity and ability that may not be attended to specifically within the choreography itself.

Thinking about Lecavalier's body, its delineated muscles and fierce physicality, as well as its position within Lock's spectacle, brings us right up against one of the most ferociously contested issues in feminist and cultural studies today. What is the status of the female body? Is it entirely a product of social discourse, or is there a pre-cultural body that is connected to a natural realm of human existence? During the 1980s, feminist theory focused these questions in terms of a central debate between essentialism and constructivism. Diana Fuss's succinct book *Essentially Speaking* is a useful primer on this issue. She defines the theoretical differences in the following manner:

For the essentialist, the body occupies a pure, pre-social, pre-discursive space. The body is "real," accessible, and transparent; it is always there and directly inter-pretable through the senses. For the constructionist, the body is never simply there, rather it is composed of a network of effects continually subject to sociopolitical determination. The body is "always already" culturally mapped; it never exists in a pure or uncoded state.[3]

Over the course of her book, Fuss deconstructs the oppositional position of each ideology, suggesting that essentialist thinking underlies the constructivist viewpoint and vice versa. She wonders, finally, whether "it may be time to ask whether essences can change and whether constructions can be normative." (p. 6) Her point is well-taken. Modern dance, for instance, was founded on a rhetoric of the "natural" (barefoot, uncorseted) female body. Yet modern dance actually (although often unselfconsciously) deconstructs its own essentialist ideology by codifying and teaching movement forms and techniques that are said to be more *natural* than other kinds of dance training. What becomes clear to the student involved in modern or contemporary dance forms which empha-size the "natural" body, is that this is a very conscious construction, one that, in fact, takes years to fully embody. It feels quite different from one's everyday experience of corporeality. On the other hand, feminist theories about the female body often have a strongly deter-ministic tone, one that suggests that since this body is "always already" mapped out, there is little room for resistance or change. These works tend to assume that the socialized body is an *essential* characteristic of our experience.

Of course, the body is precisely the place where these two realms interact. It is the place where sensation, representation, and physi-cal experiences are interpreted both symbolically and somatically. I would like to shift the terms of this debate from arguments over whether the body is either a natural or social product, to an investi-gation of the how, the process through which bodies make and are made by cultures. This focus on the *process* of embodiment rather than the *product* of a particular kind of body allows me to under-stand the ways bodies and cultures are mutually formative, but at the same time it helps me to avoid the depressingly deterministic effects of many contemporary discussions of the regulated or sub-missive body.

As an artform that relies on the body to enact its own representation, dance is one of the most intriguing and yet underexplored technologies of the female body. Dance techniques not only condition the dancers' bodies, they literally inscribe a physical ideology into dancers' physiques. The intensive daily training and performing can often radically reshape these bodies. And yet dance is certainly not *only* a discipline of the body. Anyone who has ever spent any time training to be a dancer knows in their bones and muscles that the body is restructured through physical practice, and that that physical practice has psychic consequences. Behind every different aesthetic orientation and style of movement within the field of dance, dwells a view about the world that is transmitted (albeit often subconsciously) along with the dance technique. The physical training takes place in a social situation, and the dance teacher and choreographer need to rely on verbal instructions and metaphoric images as well as the examples of their own dancing to convey the precise style and quality of movement they are interested in seeing.

These physical and verbal discourses concerning form, style, beauty, movement phrasing, and the like, combine to create a powerful ideology which can dramatically affect a dancer's subjectivity. This is most obvious in the more traditional genres of dance such as classical ballet, in which the construction of an idealized image of the female body has a long (and tortured) history, one that has been amply documented by historians, writers, artists, and choreographers, as well as dancers. Indeed, over the last fifteen years, the dance field has become increasingly conscious of the often debilitating effects (including body image problems, eating disorders, drug abuse, etc.) of the quest to embody such an image. Although most modern and contemporary dance forms have consciously expanded such a narrow image of the dancer cum ballerina (thin, graceful, feminine, white), they also create specific world views which are grounded in the physical contours of the body. I am interested in probing what ideologies are represented in works that display energized female bodies like that of Louise Lecavalier. I want to focus here on the question of how bodies and their social identities are dialectically constructed through physical practices that directly challenge traditional models of female dancing. In other words, is being physically powerful necessarily empowering for women in contemporary dance?

In dance, the choreographer uses human bodies to create physical experiences and theatrical images that exist in a world of her/his own making. The presentation of those bodies carries meaning regardless of the narrative or conceptual theme of the dance. Are these bodies grounded or do they sustain an image of lightness throughout the dance? Do they use a lot of space, or is their movement contained, bound to their body by some unknown force? Anyone even slightly familiar with the origins of modern dance in America cannot fail to remark on the sheer excessiveness of its liberatory rhetoric and the passion with which seminal figures such as Isadora Duncan condemned the artifice and repressiveness of ballet. Sometimes the physical being-in-the-world of the dancer's body and the artistic representation of that body reinforce one another to render a relatively seamless image in performance. I think of Martha Graham's use of contraction and release in her early work as a good example of this physical and metaphysical coherence. At other times, however, there can be a disjunction between the dancer's physicality and what that movement represents. In Lecavalier's dancing, for instance, there is an intriguing slippage between her muscular strength and the representation of that physicality, and this jagged edge has everything to do with gender.

As its title suggests, *Infante, C'est Destroy* relies on the iconography of heavy metal rock concerts and videos, mimicing this genre's use of fantasy, androgyny, metal armoring, phallic imagery (such as guitars, mike stands, and swords), and a certain amount of implied violence. At once both dancing rock star and imagistic muse, Lecavalier occupies two contradictory positions within the spectacle as a whole. When she is dancing live onstage, she seems to control the sequence of events, jerking her partners into action or calling off the dancing by walking off the stage. Here, Lecavalier looks and acts like a male metal star, strutting, talking back to the audience, thrashing around the stage. Similarly, her shaggy hair style and tight leather clothing are clearly related to a metal aesthetic. By vamping a hypermasculinity all the while displaying her dancing body to the audience, Lecavalier embodies the same paradox that Robert Walser identifies as a crucial component of the appeal of heavy metal to a diverse, largely male audience. In his book *Running With The Devil: Power, Gender, and Madness in Heavy Metal Music* Walser explains this contradictory position by invoking Orpheus. "But his story contains a built-in contradiction: Orpheus must sing in such a way as to demonstrate his rhetorical mastery of the world, yet such elaborate vocal display threatens to undermine

Orpheus's masculine identity. Flamboyant display of his emotions is required as evidence of his manipulative powers, but excess makes him into an object of display himself."[4]

For Lecavalier, the contradiction embedded in being at once subject of the show and object of the gaze (the choreographer's, her partner's, the audience's), is amplified in the film sequences of the spectacle. Projected on an enormous scrim at the front of the stage, the film shows Lecavalier at first clothed in a medieval suit of armor, complete with sword, and then later falling naked through a vast bleak space. There is no coherent narrative in this short film. Jumpcuts inexplicably move Lecavalier from knight in armor, to slain figure bleeding, to a Christ-like transcendence. She is alternately the aggressor, victim, and saint, all the while imaged in larger than life celluloid. Iconographically, the dual position is not that unusual in the late twentieth century, but what makes this example particularly striking is the fact that Lecavalier has literally (as well as metaphorically) inscribed both genders onto her dancing body. She not only occupies both subject and object positions with the spectacle, she embodies them, physicalizing a liminal territory that challenges what we know about the traditionally gendered body in dance.

When I showed a video of *Infante, C'est Destroy* during a conference presentation, a number of audience members who were not familiar with Lecavalier thought that she was a he. Indeed, even after I had presented my paper, some people were still incredulous that this was a female body, believing that her body was too muscular to be that of a woman.[5] Although a close movement analysis reveals just how typically gendered Lecavalier's dancing really is, it is important not to overlook how radical her physique is for many people. Delineated muscles on women's bodies obviously question some very viseral beliefs about bodies and their appropriate(d) genders. I am interested in how we read muscles as marks of strength and how this affects our reading of the female body. As my discussion of Lecavalier's dancing shows, it would be wrong immediately to assume that this muscling of women dancers' bodies is inherently liberatory.

During the past decade, there has been a virtual explosion of dances that use upper body strength, particularly in women, and require the stamina to endure unprecedented athletic challenges. The romanticized image of the ballerina as an embodiment of feminine grace and beauty, or even the image of the early modern dancer poised proud and tall in her weighted stance, has been displaced by a fearless, aerobicized physicality not unlike that of Lecavalier. Now it is not uncommon to see both women and men vaulting horizontally across the stage, catching themselves with their arms and rolling down through their chests to arch back into a diagonal one-handed handspring which takes them only momentarily to their feet before they dive across the space again. Lecavalier's dancing is one such example.

The elaborate technological spectacle and punk-chic style of La La La Human Steps has obvious roots in mega rock shows. This kind of intense, driven movement can also be seen in the work of other companies, particularly contemporary European-based, or European-influenced dance/theater groups such as the British collective DV8, the work of AnneTeresa de Keersmaeker *Rosas*, and Les Ballets Contemporaines de la Belgique. These are only a few of the companies working in this genre of Euro crash and burn dancing. The hyper-physical dancing of recent years is not, of course, unrelated to the fitness craze of the 80s which radically changed contemporary notions of what a strong, healthy body looks like.

Over the last twenty years, the fit and muscular body has become a privileged icon in contemporary American culture. Thirty years ago, it would have been unheard of for most middle class women to have desired clearly defined arm muscles. Today, delineated biceps are *de rigeur*. For the first time in Western history women are entering athletic clubs (traditionally bastions of homosocial bonding) in droves to "work out" with the nautilus machines, universal gyms, and free weights. Given the ways that women's bodies have been physically constrained and historically represented as "naturally" passive and "weak," there can be no denying that sensing the rush of adrenelin and the aliveness of one's body after exercising is a new and incredibly powerful experience. One of the most pervasive beliefs in our current culture is that building a fit and firm body, i.e. building muscles, is tantamount to building one's self-confidence. Although for some people this may be right on the mark, it is important, nonetheless, to probe the popular myths which represent muscles as empowering (especially for women), in order to examine the somatic results of weight lifting. We need to ask: What are the physical effects of this kind of training? What kinds of movement priorities does it set up?

In her work on the physical attributes of gender conditioning, Iris Young tries to articulate the phenomenological basis for feminine bodily comportment by distinguishing three modalities of feminine movement: ambiguous transcendence, inhibited intentionality, and discontinuous unity. Basically, this is fancy philosophical language for throwing like a girl, which is to say using a body part in a manner that is totally disconnected from the rest of one's weight and strength. By analyzing the ways that young girls and women are trained *not* to take up the space around them, *not* to use the capacity of their whole body when engaging in physical activity, and *not* to fully project their physical intentions onto the world around them, Young describes the tensions between experiencing one's body as both a thing and as capacity for action, as both a passive object and an active subject. "According to Merleau-Ponty, for the body to exist as a transcendent presence to the world and the immediate enactment of intentions, it cannot exist as a object. As subject, the body is referred not onto itself, but onto the world's possibilities ... . The three contradictory modalities of feminine bodily existence ... have their root, however, in the fact that for feminine existence the body frequently is both subject and object for itself as the same time and in reference to the same act."[6]

This very tension, which has also been articulated by art historians as the tension between looking and being looked at, gives us another perspective on the central paradox of women's body building competitions in which women's muscles don't function as a product of physical intention, but rather as a new style of spectacle.[7] At first, dancers such as Lecavalier would seem to escape this condition of a strong but static physicality. After all, not only are their bodies incredibly built-up, but also they use those muscles to accomplish extraordinary physical acts. Yet at the same time, the tension between experiencing the body as a thing and as a capacity for action (as an object as well as a source of agency) that Young describes as a critical underlying component of female bodily comportment is still embedded in their physical being-in-the-world. In spite of their strength and physical prowess, intensely muscled women dancers often move in an oddly distanced, object-like manner, often giving one the impression that they are manic, self-propelled rag dolls.

Let us return now to *Infante, C'est Destroy,* in order to review Lecavalier's dancing within the framework of Young's insights about the female body's being-in-the-gendered-world. Although Lecavalier is clearly the main figure onstage, ironically, her dancing presence doesn't create a sense of agency. It is true that Lecavalier's dancing is awesome (I would guess that Lecavalier has more developed muscles than her male counterparts—but since they are invariably dressed in a buttoned-up shirt, long pants and a jacket, one can only speculate), but there is also a distractingly manic edge in her movement, that can easily translate into just another representation of female hysteria. Even though Lecavalier is the keystone of the spectacle, even though she is dancing the hardest, breathing and sweating the most, she still exhibits the existential ambiguity that Young describes as a trait of female bodily comportment. A close reading of her movement will help us to discover why.[8]

Infante, C'est Destroy begins with a drum solo. The pounding drum is soon joined by a squealing guitar as the lights fade up on Lecavalier and her partner standing still. Even in this brief moment of stillness, Lecavalier's stance is far less relaxed and weighted than that of her male counterpart. Like a racehorse who is too anxious at the gate, Lecavalier is drawing all her energy into her body. Because she is so bound up, her first movements seem like mini explosions, with her hair and limbs flying like bits of shrapnel all over the place. The music is pushing her to a frenetic pace such that she always seems to take off and land on either side of the downbeat. This creates a slightly frustrating sense of her never quite being there with the music. Her movement is not just fast; it seems rushed, almost driven by an outside force. This manic quality in her dancing has a lot to do with the fact that she rarely releases her weight into the floor. Even when she is not engaging in full-body activities such as vaulting or rolling across the stage, even when she is sitting on top of her partner who is sprawled out on the floor, something is going on in her body: her head is shaking furiously; her arms are circling or punching the space in front of her; or her feet are doing little tippy-toe steps.

Much of this frenzied, almost chaotic movement seems pointless; it doesn't affect the space around her or her partner's motions, and it rarely has any rhythmic relationship to the music. There are times when she quickly performs a series of arm gestures, something like condensed semaphores, that seem to enact some sort of mysterious, ritualized act. Yet, those gestures never expand beyond a very limited space around her body, making them into a bizarrely private act. Lecavalier's movements rarely extend out beyond her own limited reach space to affect the stage space, the theatrical space of the world around her. For instance, when she does an arabesque, her leg abruptly kicks up behind her body and then drops back with no spatial intention. Her movement never extends through the space, and her gestures often refer back to her own body, even when she is grabbing or pulling her partner. It is as if she reaches out only to retract into herself. This is particularly striking given the enormous stage on which *Infante, C'est Destroy* was performed at the International Festival of New Dance.

I would identify much of Lecavalier's dancing as a prime example of Young's "discontinuous unity," particularly in terms of her use of space and weight. Her body tends to move as a series of disconnected parts. Often, an arm thrown behind her body doesn't motivate a turn in that direction, or even a wind up to turn in another direction, but rather is simply thrown out and then flops back wherever it lands. It seems as if Lecavalier looses the connection with her limbs once they are launched. Because she lets go of any spatial intention in her movement, her dancing can take on a brutal, almost masochistic quality. After a while, she seems to be just throwing her body up in the air, not particularly caring where it lands.

There are exceptions, of course. In a trio with the two other women, there is a much more lyrical quality to her dancing. Their partnering has a more relaxed, almost embracing feel about it, and there is no sense of rough competitiveness that underlies Lecavalier's duets with men. Likewise, the enormous video of Lecavalier, naked, falling in slow motion has a peaceful, almost religiously estatic quality to it. Still, at the end of this seventy-five minute spectacle, I had a very conflicted sense of Lecavalier's (not to mention Lock's) whole attitude towards her own body. On the one hand, I was astounded by the daring and physical audacity of her movement and I wondered if I could ever train to be tight enough and strong enough to do similar feats. On the other hand, I realized the sheer vulnerability of her body put under that kind of physical stress. During one performance of *Infante, C'est Destroy,* Lecavalier reportedly dislocated her hip, but only stopped dancing once the spectacle was over. This disturbing sense of disconnection in regard to her physicality is alluded to in an interview in which Lecavalier is quoted as saying, "to me, all dance is violent to the body...dancers are always pushing their bodies to do excessive things."[9]

By analyzing her actual physical movements as well as her position within the spectacle as a whole, I am arguing for a more complex awareness of how dance operates as a form of representation.

I believe that it is important not only to look at the narrative, icono-graphic gestures, symbolic images, and social relationships within the choreography, but also to recognize how meaning is literally embodied in the dancer's physicality. As mysterious as it may seem to the audience, I believe a performer's theatrical persona is grounded in the realities of weight, space, and movement inten-tionality, the dancer's literal being-in-the-world. While we may not be entirely conscious of these elements within a performance, they undoubtedly effect how we perceive the dancing as well as the dancers. What is intriguing in the example of Lecavalier's dancing is the way that her visible musculature and powerful dancing contradicts her gendered use of space and weight within Lock's rock spectacle. While her built-up body radically challenges a conventionally feminine body or movement style, Lecavalier's dis-connected intentionality reinforces her traditionally gendered role. Because Lecavalier's dancing produces these physical attributes simultaneously, her theatrical presence remains an enigma, at once refusing and yet enacting the bodily codes of gender.

Notes

1. La La La Human Steps Press Packet, 1993.
2. Judith Butler, *Gender Trouble: Feminism and the Subversion of Identity*, New York: Routledge Press, 1990, p. 93.
3. Diana Fuss, *Essentially Speaking: Feminism, Nature and Difference*, New York: Routledge Press, 1989, pp. 5–6.
4. Robert Walser, *Running with the Devil: Power, Gender and Madness in Heavy Metal Music*, Hanover, Wesleyan University Press, 1993, p. 108.
5. At the fall 1994 CORD conference, an arguement broke out about whether Lecavalier could build-up to this heightened muscularity without the use of ste-riods. What interests me here is not whether she uses steriods or not, but the fact that her body so profoundly disturbs our notions of the "natural" female body that even progressive feminists found themselves arguing that Lacavalier needed drugs to alter her "natural" body so fundamentally.
6. Iris Young, *Throwing Like a Girl and Other Essays in Feminist Philosophy and Social Theory*, Bloomington: Indiana University Press, 1990, p. 123 and 150.
7. For a more in-depth discussion of power, gender, and spectacle in women's body building see Chapter 2 in my recent book, *Choreographing Difference: The Body and Identity in Contemporary Dance*.
8. The following detailed analysis of Lacavalier's movement style would have been impossible without the generosity of the company in lending me a video tape of several sections of the spectacle. I am deeply grateful to Anne Viau for accomo-dating my request.
9. Quote from The Gazette 1/15/92, contained in La La La Human Steps Press Packet.

Choreography and Dance
1998, Vol. 5, Part 1, pp. 53–70
Photocopying permitted by license only

For Men or Women? The Case of *Chinju kŏmmu*, a Sword Dance from South Korea

Judy Van Zile

In 1967 *Chinju kŏmmu*, or the Sword Dance of the City of Chinju, was designated an Intangible Cultural Asset by the government of South Korea. At that time its choreography was fixed and it was established as a dance for eight women, although the dance is said to have been originated by men. The article examines the historical development of *Chinju kŏmmu* from the perspective of the gender of its performers and the functions the dance has served at different times. This is followed by a discussion of movement characteristics. The author proposes that although the dance, as performed today, retains clear suggestions of both male–female and masculine–feminine characteristics, and while features of these dichotomous categories have contributed to the development of the dance and, indeed, to its very survival, ultimately gender is not what the dance is about.

KEY WORDS Gender, Korean dance, sword dance, *kisaeng* (female entertainers).

Eight female dancers walk casually into the performing space.[1] They wear long blue skirts and long-sleeved blouses. Atop this traditional clothing of Korean women, they wear long dark blue jackets styled after those of male military officials of former times. Each dancer's hair is pulled back tightly at the nape of the neck into a chignon, through which is thrust a long hair pin—both typical of older Korean women. On top of their heads they sport round, flat, black hats, each with a peacock feather and red tassle dropping lazily over the side and a chain of large red and yellow beads draped loosely beneath the chin—again reminiscent of former male military attire. The dancers' long, multicolored sleeves, typical of female court dancers of an earlier era, hang almost to the ground, and each hand grasps a specially-made sword not much longer than a dagger. Small metal ornaments dangle loosely from the blade and a red tassle is suspended from the handle, a design that contributes to the swords' aesthetic rather than realistic function.

The dancers position themselves in two lines facing each other, both lines perpendicular to the audience. They slowly lower themselves to a kneel, quietly place their swords on the ground beside them, and rise to begin the dance.

They continually bend and extend their knees as they walk slowly through a series of formations in which the lines merge, open into two lines parallel to the audience, and merge and open several more times. They then remove the long sleeves fastened at their wrists and drop them to the floor at the sides of the performing area.

Again the dancers change their group formation, this time moving their hands and wrists as if holding and manipulating the swords.

Upon re-forming their original two parallel lines they sit, grasp the long "tails" of their jackets, and move them to reveal the red inner lining. The dancers then tie the ends of their jacket tails behind their backs, and, while still seated, move their hands and wrists once more as if holding and manipulating the swords.

They pick up one sword and then the other, and flick their wrists while bending and extending their elbows and turning their forearms. The metal ornaments on the swords clang gently and the tassles spin as the blades trace arcs in space, movements that are ornamental rather than realistic representations of combat actions.

The dancers stand and change formations again, continuing to manipulate the swords as they advance and retreat, and then form a circle.

By this time the tempo has increased and the dancers do a series of individual turns at the same time they progress around the circle, all the while continuing the complex arm movement and wrist flicking. The turns are reminiscent of movements most often seen in dances performed by men and the concurrent sword manipulation ornaments the movement rather than replicating fighting actions.

The tempo then slows, the dancers walk around the circle, still manipulating their swords, form a single straight line parallel to the audience, bow, and quietly exit by backing away from the performing area.

No story has been told. Only a hint of military action has been offered. The strongest impression is that of a kaleidoscopic ensemble

Figure 9   A group formation early in the dance.

of women who perform in unison, gently grouping and regrouping amidst a calm swishing of sword blades—all with a serious and slightly weighty quality.

This twenty-minute dance is most frequently identified as *Chinju kŏmmu*. *Kŏm* is the Korean word for "sword" and *mu* the Sino-Korean word for "dance." Throughout history there have been many sword dances in Korea, all of which are known generically as *kŏmmu*. Although historical documentation has clouded the precise origin of these dances, today the small city of Chinju, near the southern tip of the South Korean peninsula, is considered the home of a sword dance given special recognition by the Korean government, and referred to as *Chinju kŏmmu*.[2]

Following is an outline of the history of *Chinju kŏmmu*[3] and an examination of the dance in relation to gender. A conclusion is drawn that although the dance, as performed today, retains clear suggestions of both male–female and masculine–feminine characteristics,[4] and while features of these dichotomous categories have contributed to the development of the dance, indeed, to its very survival, gender is not what the dance is ultimately about.

The early history of Korean sword dances liberally intertwines fact and fiction. An historical text compiled in the late 1600s (*T'ongyŏng chapki*) documents two stories dating from as early as 660 A.D. There are differences in the stories, but they both relate to a young boy from the Silla Kingdom. In one story he was sent to the enemy kingdom of Paekche to dance in the streets. The king of Paekche heard of the beauty of the young boy's dancing and invited him to perform in the court. While performing a sword dance before the king, the young boy seized the opportunity to help his homeland by killing the enemy king with his dance weapons. He was then captured and executed. According to this story, the people in his homeland of Silla created a mask with his features and performed a sword dance to commemorate their young dancer–hero's courageous act.

The second story simply indicates that a young boy soldier was killed in battle. In sorrow, his father made a mask of the boy's face, and during funeral rituals the boy's fellow soldiers performed a sword dance. (It is not clear if the dancers in either story actually wore masks during the dance.)

The most significant commonalities in these stories in relation to *Chinju kŏmmu* are the tie to military personnel and battle, the use of a sword, and the indication that the earliest sword dance performers were boys or men. (The original dance in the first story was performed by a young boy; it is not clear, in that story, whether the people who danced to commemorate the death of the young boy dancer were male or female. The fellow soldiers who danced in the second story were undoubtedly men.) Historical records are not adequate to trace completely the development of sword dances, but we do know that changes occurred in the number and gender of the performers.

For more than a century following the written documentation of their origin, references to sword dances are minimal, with significant ones not appearing until the 19th century. At that time official records documented formal court activities and included information comparable to elaborate program notes. These and other records mention sword dances and/or include line drawings of them.[5] Some of the drawings show four female dancers and others two male dancers.

One of the richest descriptions of sword dance movements is contained in an 1896 publication by a foreigner that briefly describes a dance performed at the royal court in Seoul.

The dancers are as usual clothed in voluminous garments of striking colors. Long and brilliantly colored sleeves reach down to and beyond the hand. False hair is added to make an elaborate headdress in which many gay ornaments are fastened. The dance is done in stockinged feet, and as the sword dance is the most lively of all, robes are caught up and the sleeves turned back out of the way. The girls pirouette between swords laid on the floor and as the music becomes more lively they bend to one side and the other near the swords until at last they have them in their hands, then the music quickens and the swords flash this way and that as the dancer wheels and glides about in graceful motion. A good dancer will work so fast and twirl her swords so dexterously as to give one the impression that the blade must have passed through her neck. This dance is also done in men's clothes at times, but the cut of the garments of the sexes is so much alike as to present little external difference except that the colors of the men's are either white or of one shade, and the mass of hair worn by the dancer ordinarily is replaced by a simple hat. (Allen, 1896: 384)

This passage is particularly interesting because of its comments regarding the male *or* female attire worn by female dancers. Today's costume includes components of attire worn by women *as well as* those worn by men. The movement dynamics described by Allen, however, are in direct contrast to the version of *Chinju kŏmmu* performed today and described at the beginning of this article.

Despite the probability that men or boys were the earliest performers of sword dances, today the primary performers and teachers of *Chinju kŏmmu* are women in the city of Chinju who have been designated by the Korean government to perpetuate the dance. Although perhaps originally performed for ritual or celebratory purposes, *Chinju kŏmmu* is performed today primarily for entertainment or to display cultural manifestations of Korea's past. It is done in the capital of Seoul as part of special performances of dance and music that have been designated Intangible Cultural Assets, occasionally in concert performances of traditional dance and music throughout South Korea, and, most importantly, in Chinju at an annual festival to honor a woman known as Nongae.

Nongae became a heroine in Chinju in the late sixteenth century. The city played a pivotal role in Korean battles with the Japanese, and despite attempts to maintain its stand, ultimately succumbed, on several occasions, to the powerful blows of its island neighbor. Because of her reputation as an entertainer (known as a *kisaeng*[6]), in October of 1592 Nongae's presence was requested at a Japanese victory celebration held inside the Chinju castle. Although she graciously met her obligation to fill the leisure time of the Japanese officials, she maintained her loyalty to Korea and privately lamented the death of her Korean sponsor. She lured the Japanese general she was entertaining to a precipice overlooking the Nam River, which runs through the city of Chinju. To show her support for her homeland, while embracing him in an assumed air of affection she pulled him over the brink to their mutual deaths in the water below. In time a shrine was erected along the river at the site where the incident took place, and an annual festival is now held to honor Nongae. What is particularly intriguing in relation to gender is that at this festival to honor a woman, eight women clad in costumes based on male military attire perform a dance with roots that apparently lie in a dance of men, with movement qualities that although suggestive, have been transformed to a quality more appropriate to women.

The quality of the movements used in today's *Chinju kŏmmu* is predominantly soft and gentle, characteristics that epitomized femininity in the Confucian-dominated Chosŏn courts (1392–1910).[7] This quality is sometimes layered on top of less feminine movements, such as exposing the palms of the hands. Korean court women did not expose this part of their bodies. It is likely this contributed to dance movements in which arm gestures are seldom complete until the forearm turns inward and the wrist relaxes so the fingertips point gently downward, concealing the palm. Hence, if the palms

are shown, it is only in passing. Some Korean scholars also believe
the desire to conceal the palms contributed to female court dancers
covering their hands with long sleeves. Movements concealing the
palm are present in *Chinju kŏmmu*, as is the use of long sleeves to
hide the hands. But early in the dance the sleeves are removed and
in one section of the dance a gentle, but nonetheless blatant, display
of the palms is performed—a movement not found in any other
Korean dance.[8]

The "palm display" movement of *Chinju kŏmmu* begins with one
arm extended forward at shoulder height and the other overhead,
both turned so the palms face upward. (Figure 10) The fingers are
laterally closed and rounded so that the palm surfaces of the fingers
lightly touch the palm surface of the thumb. The fingers then open
and straighten quickly, exposing the palms, before the arms begin
excursions through the horizontal and vertical planes: as the forward arm opens sideward at shoulder height, the high arm lowers
down to the side of the body.

A *Chinju kŏmmu* movement that is particularly unusual among
traditional Korean dances and that is also counter to stereotypic
Confucian female decorum is one that might be called the "torso
display." (Figure 11) Although the arms are often extended sideward
at shoulder height in Korean dances performed by women, there is
a tendency to move them forward a bit so they point slightly to the
diagonal rather than sideward, and to round the shoulders a little to
make the front surface of the chest slightly concave, de-emphasizing
the female anatomy. In *Chinju kŏmmu*, however, there is a movement that opens out the chest area. In one sequence the dancers
rather abruptly assume a fourth position and tilt their torsos back-
ward with their arms opened sideward at shoulder height, the
palms again facing upward. This movement, which blatantly opens
out the front surface of the dancers' bodies, is the direct antithesis
of the traditional humble and gentle female deportment.

No one knows for sure the reason for these movements, unusual
for Korean women as well as for Korean dance in general, nor any
meaning that may have been derived from them. Nor does anyone
know when such unusual movements became a part of *Chinju
kŏmmu*. While there are several possible explanations, all of them
are speculative. One native Korean dance researcher believes that
the palm displaying movement was present in dances performed in
the court during the Chosŏn dynasty, and that this movement has
been preserved *only* in *Chinju kŏmmu*. In former times court dances

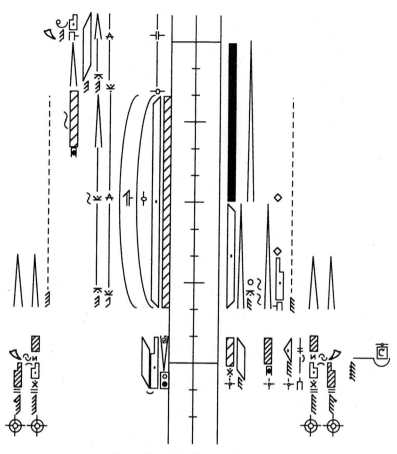

Figure 10   Palm Display Movement.

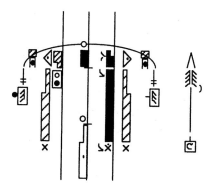

Figure 11   Torso Display Movement.

were sometimes performed by men, and, as previously mentioned, several illustrations substantiate this. Therefore, it is possible this type of movement was originally appropriately performed by male court dancers, and was not transformed when women began to perform the dance. Thus, it is possible that *Chinju kŏmmu*, as performed today, retains movements originally performed in the court by male dancers, and that the dance was originally a court dance.

A second possibility, expressed by a Chinju dance teacher, relates to the story of the origin of the dance. She feels the displaying of the palms and chest area are very strong, courageous movements and are an attempt to incorporate into the dance a sense of the strength and courage of the young boy dancer who killed the enemy king. If this is accurate, the origin and meaning of the dance may have provided acceptable reasons for women to perform movements that otherwise would have been unacceptable.

A third possibility lies in the Chinju environment in which the dance performed today is said to have evolved or to have been preserved. Because the dance was originally perpetuated in this region by *kisaeng*, the dancers, either because of their artistic or their social functions, may have been allowed to take liberties with movement and the display of their bodies inappropriate for other women. This explanation is tenuous, however, in light of the notion that the use of long sleeves by court dancers who were *kisaeng* may have originated in the inappropriateness of women showing their hands before the king. Would not a *kisaeng* show a similar respect to patrons outside the court?

A fourth possibility is that standards of female propriety inhibiting the display of the palms and chest area were imposed during the Chosŏn dynasty, with its strong Confucian ideals. If this is the case, movements displaying these body parts may be indicative of a considerably older dance style, a style preserved today only in *Chinju kŏmmu*.

The notion of *Chinju kŏmmu* pre-dating the Chosŏn period is supported in a governmental report submitted in 1966. This document justifies the government's designating *Chinju kŏmmu* an Intangible Cultural Asset by asserting that although there were many versions of sword dances performed at the time the report was written, and although the Chinju version had changed the overall movements from harsh to soft and graceful,[9] the Chinju version was the most "authentic".[10] The report goes on to state that during the Chosŏn period two versions of a sword dance were performed in the royal court: one by male dancers for a male audience; the other by female dancers for a female audience.[11] Furthermore, the 1966 report, together with subsequent documentation and the memories of older dancers alive in the 1980s, clearly establishes women as the performers, since the early 1900s, of what is now known as *Chinju kŏmmu*. The earliest of these female performers were *kisaeng*.

By the time of the Koryŏ period (918–1392), Korea had established a tradition (believed by many to have been patterned after a practice in T'ang China) of female court entertainers. This institution of female entertainers involved a hierarchy of women who served in unofficial and official capacities with the local and/or central government. Various titles indicated the status of these women, based on their abilities and government affiliation, with *"kisaeng"* being the general term for "female entertainer". The highest ranking *kisaeng* were those affiliated with the highest level of government.

During the Chosŏn dynasty there were twelve official *kisaeng* unions established in major provincial government areas to train young women entertainers for government officials in the provinces as well as for large, important banquets of the central government. One union was located in the city of Chinju. Although administrative authority for the training of *kisaeng* originally belonged to the royal court, this function was taken over by regional private schools in the early 1900s. These schools taught their own specialities, such as literature, music, or dance (Lee Byong-won, 1979: 80), and the sword dance known today as *Chinju kŏmmu* became the speciality of the *kisaeng* school in Chinju.

According to former *kisaeng* alive in the early 1980s, and in reference to a time period probably in the mid-1930s, the Chinju Female Entertainers' Union (Chinju Kisaeng Chohap) held a kind of workshop (*sasŭp*) for seven days every March. At one of these workshops dancers were specifically recruited to learn a sword dance. Thirty to forty women applied and began the seven-day session, but many dropped out because of the difficulty of some portions of the dance.

The portion considered to be most difficult was the "flying" part near the end of the dance. This movement done by male dancers in some Korean dances is essentially a barrel turn in which the dancer jumps high off the ground while turning. This same movement has been modified in *Chinju kŏmmu* so that the dancers do not leave the ground. The modification better suits models of stereotypic Confucian Korean feminine decorum, but retains the essence of the more vigorous movement, more usually associated with male dancers, from which it derives.[12]

At the conclusion of the seven-day training period, four of the remaining women were chosen to perform.

From some time after this workshop until the end of the Korean War (1950–1953), *Chinju kŏmmu* was not performed; however, in the late 1950s, it was revived. Two major changes are known to have occurred in the sword dance performed by *kisaeng* in Chinju before the 1930s and after the Korean War: eight women began to perform the dance instead of four, and the dance was considerably shortened. Older dancers state that the dance originally took one hour to perform; the full version performed today lasts approximately 20 minutes.

These two changes came about largely through the efforts of Pak Hŏn-bong (1907–1977, also known as Ki San), an avid supporter of the performing arts. Although not an artist himself, Pak was a strong advocate of folk traditions and strove to preserve Korean folk culture. In the late 1950s Pak requested that eight women reconstruct the Chinju sword dance. (There is no indication as to why he requested eight performers.) According to one of the female dancers involved in the reconstruction,[13] it was not difficult to bring the dance to life again. In spite of the fact that it had not been performed since the mid-1930s, it was still very much alive in the women's memories because they had performed it so many times. Pak was then instrumental in having *Chinju p'al kŏmmu*[14] designated an Intangible Cultural Asset in 1967.

In preparation for bestowing the governmental honor and because of the advancing age of the early *Chinju kŏmmu* performers, a cultural institute in Chinju recruited women for a special workshop in 1966. These women were specifically to learn and carry on the tradition of *Chinju kŏmmu*. In 1967 eight women were designated National Living Treasures whose responsibility was to perpetuate the dance. Four of the women were those originally selected from the entertainers' union to perform in the mid-1930s and four were "second generation" dancers selected from the 1966 workshop. A third generation of dancers was subsequently selected from individuals who responded to a recruiting scheme that focused on middle-aged housewives. This group was specifically targeted rather than younger women because of the fear that younger women would leave Chinju to marry or attend college, and hence would not contribute to the preservation of the dance. These training sessions, financed by the city and offered free to participants, were initially attended by 50 women, but attrition was high. As in the mid-1930s *kisaeng* workshop, drop-outs cited the difficulty of the dance as a major reason; some also believed it was inappropriate for women to spend as much time away from home as was necessary to learn the dance. Confucian notions of the place of women and the low stature of *kisaeng* had left indelible marks.[15]

The focus on middle-aged housewives points to a significant difference between the first generation of clearly identifiable female dancers and those of later generations: the first generation were all professional entertainers who had learned a number of arts skills; from at least the third generation on, the dancers were housewives who were not professionals and whose arts skills focused specifically on *Chinju kŏmmu*. The third generation maintained their positions as housewives while simultaneously assuming their roles as perpetuators of *Chinju kŏmmu*. Hence, at the same time they continued the stereotypic role of the woman belonging to the house, they were entrusted with the perpetuation of one of Korea's officially-designated cultural artifacts and were in positions of significant recognition.

The primary administrative force behind the perpetuation of *Chinju kŏmmu* in the 1990s is Song Kae-ok, one of the "second generation" of dancers who was eventually designated by the Korean government as one of the eight highest ranking perpetuators of the dance. Her involvement with the dance reflects a number of things relating to gender and societal attitudes. Because of a strict Confucian upbringing, Song spent her early days studying Chinese literature. Her parents maintained the commonly held belief that dance was performed by female entertainers, whose status was quite low despite their importance in government functions. (It is interesting to note that during the Chosŏn period, which ended shortly before Song was born, Confucianism prevented women from most forms of education and many women were illiterate. It was the *kisaeng* who were the primary female "readers and writers.") Although she had a keen interest in dance, it was not until her husband died that Song began to study it. She was then torn between her freedom to learn dance and her family obligation to support her five children. The latter necessity led to developing a strong business sense, and it was not until the mid-1970s that she became actively involved with the *Chinju kŏmmu* dancers. Because of her sophisticated educational background and her business acumen, she has served as coordinator for the activities of the *Chinju kŏmmu* dancers since the 1980s.

What can we make of this rather complex and not-always-known historical background in relation to gender issues and the way *Chinju kŏmmu* is performed today? *Chinju kŏmmu*'s development has led to a dance that includes many movements stereotypically characteristic of other older Korean dances, some of which are performed primarily by women and some primarily by men. Additionally, some of the costume components are or were typically worn by women and some by men. All of these features are distinctively present rather than being combined in any androgynous manner. The intent of the dance is not primarily to represent literally its likely military origins nor to represent women or men. The 1967 designation of *Chinju kŏmmu* as an Intangible Cultural Asset was, like many other such designations, recognition of something that displayed a distinctively Korean identity without particular regard for gender representation. It was an acknowledgment of something considered important from Korea's past selected to create a Korean identity in the present, regardless of gender issues.[16]

It is intriguing that a dance attributed to male military roots is now performed to celebrate the heroic deed of a woman (Nongae) important in the history of the city of Chinju. It is also intriguing that a dance with such roots became the purview first of young female entertainers and eventually of middle-aged housewives. What is particularly fascinating from a movement perspective is why a movement associated with stronger dances most usually performed by men (the "flying" movement), and several movements that directly contradict notions of femininity prevalent in Korea at least at one time in history (the "palm display" and "torso display" movements), have been choreographed together with movements that are more stereotypically feminine. Information available today does not allow us to assign meaning to these features nor to ascertain a clear rationale for their existence; they remain a puzzle.[17]

Chinju kŏmmu may be on the brink of another change, however. In 1990, young professional women dancers of the Korean Traditional Performing Arts Center (Kungnip kugagwŏn), a government-sponsored institute in Seoul, began to perform *Chinju kŏmmu*. They modified the usually full, loose-fitting costume by wrapping the skirt tightly in a style that is traditional when women are working and want to keep their full skirt out of the way. This style reveals the contours of the female body. While for working women such a display of the female form was undoubtedly inadvertent, for the viewer of *Chinju kŏmmu* it specifically calls attention to the fact that the performers are women. And the dance these women perform has a very light, uplifting, and almost joyous quality. All of these features constitute a sharp contrast to the full-figured image of Chinju's housewife-dancers and their weighty performance quality. It is easy to envision this as the beginning of another significant change in one of Korea's officially designated dance treasures.

Notes

1. Portions of this paper are based on Van Zile, 1991a and 1991b.
2. The complete name of the dance is *Chinju p'al kŏmmu. P'al* is the Korean word for the number eight, and it is the version of the dance performed by eight women that was designated an Intangible Cultural Asset by the Korean government in 1967. (For an explanation of Korea's Intangible Cultural Asset system see Van Zile, 1987.) Although "*kŏm*" is the Korean word for "sword," the dance is frequently referred to in both Korean and English as a "knife" dance (*kal ch'um* in Korean) because of the relatively small size of the implement used today. Hence, the title of the dance indicates the city with which it is associated, the number of dancers, and the implement used in the dance. Today the dance is sometimes performed by fewer than eight dancers in an abbreviated format, so it is generally referred to simply as *Chinju kŏmmu.*
3. For a fuller historical treatment of the dance see Van Zile, 1991a.
4. The category "male–female" (or "man–woman") is used here in relation to aspects identified on the basis of physiological traits; "masculine–feminine" is used in reference to characteristics associated with non-physiological traits. For example, some dances are performed only by men and some only by women, the labels referring to physiological traits of the performers. Movements identified as "masculine" may be those most usually performed by men and hence given the appellation "masculine," but they may also be performed by women.
5. See, for example, the 1893 *Kungjung chŏngjae mudo holgi* (Written Material on Court Entertainment Dances).
6. "*Kisaeng*" is a "Chinese compound that can be loosely translated as 'students of the arts performed by females.'" "*Kisaeng* "participated in the full panoply of social events that comprised the cultural lives of Korea's governing elite. In the capital, as members of the Court Entertainment Bureau, *kisaeng* presented elaborately choreographed music and dance pieces on festival days and occasions of state, twirling long crimson sashes and carrying a dazzling array of banners emblazoned with pairs of phoenixes and peacocks; when court officials required 'willow waists' and mouth organs to foster a party mood at private banquets they were summoned out as well. At government offices throughout the provinces rosters of *kisaeng* were kept so that 'glistening eyebrows' and 'crimson skirts' would be on hand to greet visiting dignitaries and newly appointed administrators. At the end of a long night of banqueting, they might also be called upon to 'provide a pillow' and ease the loneliness of the hours remaining until dawn" (McCarthy, 1994: 6).
7. Unfortunately documentation does not allow us to know precisely how appropriate feminine decorum of the period was translated into movement. Descriptions

do, however, suggest softness, gentility, and humbleness: women were considered inferior to men; an unmarried woman followed the dictum's of her father, a married woman those of her husband, and a widowed woman those of her son; a woman was responsible for maintaining purity in customs; women were to be strong and responsible but modest and submissive; and, above all, a woman had to be virtuous (Deuchler, 1977: 3–4). A wife was to be "loyal and pure, self-controlled, flexible and obedient, and serving others. She minds exclusively the domestic realm and does not concern herself with public affairs" (Deuchler, 1993: 574). (For further comments on desirable characteristics of women during the Chosŏn period see, for example, Deuchler, 1977 and 1993, Koh, 1987, and Young Hee Lee, 1994.)

8. That this movement, known as *ip ch'um*, appears in no other Korean dance performed today and is so unlike any movement found in other Korean dances makes one wonder about its origin. Unfortunately the name given to the movement does not provide a clue. "*Ch'um*" is simply the Korean word for 'dance.' Dictionary translations and those provided by *Chinju kŏmmu* dancers indicate that "*ip*" means 'mouth,' 'tongue,' 'speech,' 'words,' 'a beak,' and 'one's taste.' While it is possible to imagine the opening of the curled fingers that displays the palm to symbolize speech, the opening of one's mouth, or the opening of a beak, this does not bear any relationship to the nature of the dance or its origin. Some senior dancers say the movement symbolizes the shooting of a bow and arrow. This is logical in relation to the military nature of the supposed origin of the dance, but is not logical when considering that the early stories all specifically describe a *sword* dance. Although not attempting to translate the words "*ip ch'um*," one important *Chinju kŏmmu* dancer describes the movement as resembling the opening of the petals of a flower (Ch'ae Yae-bun: personal communication 3/18/91).

9. Kim Ch'un-heung *et al.*, p. 27.

10. *Ibid.*, p. 10. The report describes a number of specific movement differences between the version of the dance performed in Chinju and those performed elsewhere. It is unclear, however, in describing the specific rationale for considering the Chinju version the most authentic, authenticity being an important criteria for designating dances Intangible Cultural Assets. The report refers to documentation contained in several important historical works at the same time it comments on difficulties in knowing precisely how the Chinju movements relate to those described in only general ways in some of the sources. The age and memories of dancers alive at the time the report was written seem to be the primary rationale for establishing authenticity, which is apparently equated with closeness to some original performance.

11. In both cases the dance was done by two performers (*ibid.*, p. 21).

12. According to Deuchler (1977: 4), "The Confucian image of woman was … a double one: she had to be modest and submissive, but also strong and responsible. On the level of Confucian idealism, the image was considered virtuous; on the level of daily life, it often meant bondage." This notion of women having a dual image could provide an interesting explanation for taking an essentially masculine movement and modifying it for a more feminine execution.

13. I Yun-rae (6/14/83).

14. This is the full title of the dance, as described in Note 2.

15. Views of *kisaeng* seemed to vary. While some looked down on them with great scorn and considered them a "threat to Confucian propriety" (see, for example,

McCarthy, 1994: 6), the nature of the dances they performed in the court appears to have epitomized the stereotypic notion of female Confucian propriety. They symbolically depicted the ideal while, in reality, were often accorded a far-from-ideal status.

16. For a discussion of Korea's Intangible Culture Asset system and issues of identity see Van Zile, 1995.

17. It would be tempting, for example, to attribute the less feminine (in a Confucian framework) movements to women's movements of the 1920s that were liberating women from some of the strictures of Confucianism (see, for example, Kim, 1994). But there is insufficient evidence to establish a cause-effect relationship. (For an indication of gender issues in relation to music see Howard, 1995.)

References

Allen, Horace N. (1896) "Some Korean Customs. Dancing Girls," *The Korean Repository.* Vol. III, No. 10 (October), pp. 383–386.

Deuchler, Martina (1993) "Sin Sukchu: 'House Rules'," in Peter H. Lee, editor. *Sourcebook of Korean Civilization. Vol. I. From Early Times to the Sixteenth Century.* New York: Columbia University Press, pp. 571–574.

——. (1977) "The Tradition: Women during the Yi Dynasty," in *Virtues in Conflict. Tradition and the Korean Woman Today*, Sandra Mattieli, editor. Korea: Royal Asiatic Society, Korea Branch, pp. 1–48.

Howard, Keith (1995) "Gender Issues in the Conservation of Korean Music: Some Presumptive Assumptions," in Klaus Wolfgang Niemoller, Uwe Patzold, and Kyochul Chung, editors. *Lux Oriente—Begegnungen der Kulturen in der Musikforschung: Festschrift Robert Gunther Zum 65 Geburstag.* Koln: Gustav Bosse Verlag, pp. 181–195.

Kim, Ch'un-heung, Pak Hon-bong, and Yi Ki-yong (1966) *Ch'inju kŏmmu. Muhyong munhwajae chosa pogoso* [*Chinju kŏmmu.* Intangible Cultural Asset Research Report]. Seoul: Munhwajae kwalliguk.

Kim, Yung-Hee (1994) "Women's Issues in 1920s Korea," *Korean Culture.* Vol. 15, No. 2, pp. 26–33.

Koh, Hesung Chun (1987) "Womens' Roles and Achievements in the Yi Dynasty," in *Korean Women in Transition. At Home and Abroad.* Eui-Young Yu and Earl H. Phillips, editors. California: Center for Korean-American and Korean Studies, California State University, Los Angeles, pp. 29–45.

Lee, Byong-won (1979) "Evolution of the Role and Status of Korean Professional Female Entertainers (Kisaeng)," *World of Music.* Vol. XVI, No. 2, pp. 75–81.

Lee, Young Hee (1994) "Women's Literature in the Traditional and Early Modern Periods," *Korean Culture.* Vol. 15, No. 2, pp. 14–25.

McCarthy, Kathleen (1994) "*Kisaeng* and Poetry in the Koryo Period," *Korean Culture.* Vol. 15, No. 2, pp. 4–13.

Van Zile, Judy (1995) "From Ritual to Entertainment and Back Again: The Case of *Ch'oyongmu*, a Korean Dance," *Dance, Ritual and Music. Proceedings of the 18th Symposium of the Study Group on Ethnochoreology, The International Council for Traditional Music.* Warsaw, Poland: Polish Society for Ethnochoreology Institute of Art–Polish Academy of Sciences, pp. 133–140.

——. (1991a) "Chinju's Dance Treasure," *Asiana*. Vol. 3, No. 10 (October), pp. 8–14, 16–17.

——. (1991b) *"Chinju kŏmmu:* An Implement Dance of Korea," *Studia Musicologica Academiae Scientiarum Hungaricae*, Vol. 33, Nos. 1–4, pp. 359–366.

——. (1987) "How the Korean Government Preserves Its Cultural Heritage," *Korean Culture*, Vol. 8, No. 2 (Summer), pp. 18–19.

Choreography and Dance
1998, Vol. 5, Part 1, pp. 71–78
Photocopying permitted by license only

African American Women Gender Identity and West African Dance

Phylisé Smith

West African dance became a popular cultural expression among urban African Americans during the 1960s Black Power Movement. Currently, for many African Americans especially African American women, West African dance participation is still a popular cultural expression. Focusing upon West African dance in Los Angeles African American communities, I describe how West African dance participation promotes gender and cultural self-esteem among African American women. In articulating this viewpoint, I examine the roles that African American women portray in West African dance and their views of these roles. My research methodology includes participant-observation of Los Angeles West African dance classes from 1993–1996, formal interviews with 5 West African dancers and distribution of survey questionnaires to 25 of the dancers.

Through my research, I have discovered that performing West African dance provides African American women with experiences that give them gender and cultural self-esteem. Such experiences make West African dance a necessary and significant expression of their womanhood and heritage.

KEY WORDS   African American women, gender self-esteem, cultural self-esteem, West African dance, roles of women in West African dance, West African dance, Senegalese/Guinea dance.

I have been studying, teaching, and performing West African dance in Los Angeles for 10 years.[1] During this time, I have observed that African American women enjoy performing West African dance and make up the majority of West African dance participants. I have also observed that African American women especially enjoy the roles they portray while dancing.[2] They enjoy these roles even though in West African dance, the roles of men and women and the dance environment are highly delineated. For example, in West African dance, women demonstrate their femininity while men demonstrate their virility. As a rule, women do not perform men's movements nor do the men perform women's. Rarely do women play the drum music which accompanies the dances. Men may either play drums, dance or do both.

When I first began to take West African dance classes in Los Angeles, I questioned the appeal of the female roles. But gradually, I too began to enjoy the portrayal of the "African woman" through the dance. I found I could understand what the other women were feeling while dancing. My own participation made me realize that performing West African dance provides African American women with positive experiences that contribute to what I call gender and cultural self-esteem. Gender self-esteem arises from events that allow African American women to value the fact that they are women, whereas, cultural self-esteem arises from events that allow them to value their ethnic heritage.

Given that I experience gender and cultural self-esteem when I perform West African dance and that I also have an interest in dance influences upon African American culture, I wanted to research the following; What are the exact roles African American women play in West African dance and how do these roles lead to their enjoyment of the dance? Why are African American women the majority of West African dance participants? Is there a connection between their participation and the roles they play through the dance? What do African American women think about the movements and dances they perform?

To explore these questions, I participated in and observed numerous West African dance classes from 1993–1996. I distributed survey questionnaires to 25 fellow dancers, formally interviewing 5 of them. What I found verified my personal conclusions. West African dance creates a special context for African American women that allows us to feel powerful. The dance gives us power as women and also as African Americans. These feelings of power generate gender and cultural self-esteem. It is this gender and cultural self-esteem that make West African dance a popular expression for African American women.

West African Dance in the U.S.

Richard Long (1989) notes that United States tours of authentic West African dance companies such as Keita Fodeba's Ballet

Africans sparked initial interest among African Americans in West African dance; however the real catalyst for introducing West African dance to African American communities was the 1960s Black Power Movement with slogans such as "Black is Beautiful", and "I'm Black and I'm Proud".

In Los Angeles, African American interest in West African dance was the result of post Watts riot cultural programs and the Black Nationalist movement. In 1965, a major riot devastated the Los Angeles African American community. Afterwards the City of Los Angeles vowed to assist African Americans through job and cultural programs. Because of these cultural programs, native Nigerian and Ghanaian dancers and musicians, in residence at the University of California Los Angeles, visited newly established African American community centers and taught traditional dance and music classes. African Americans eager to establish an African cultural connection began to pack these classes. By the end of the 1960s, there were many African Americans, especially African American women, not only taking classes but also performing with the Nigerian and Ghanaian artists. For example, an ensemble of Ghanaians and African Americans frequently performed in Los Angeles folk festivals.

In the 1970s, two influences changed the West African dance scene. The first influence was *Roots*, a television mini-series, based upon author Alex Haley's book, *Roots*. *Roots* was the story of Haley's search for his African ancestors. The television series which was said to have had an estimated 130 million American viewers seeing all or part of it had a profound effect upon how African Americans viewed the countries of Senegal and the Gambia. Further the lead actor in *Roots*, Levar Burton, was living in Los Angeles at the time of the movie's airing. He promoted interest in Senegal and encouraged African Americans to seek their own "roots" (Smith, 1991). The second influence was the visit of Senegalese and Guinean dancers and musicians who introduced a new and fast-paced style of dance and a different drum called the "Djimbe".[3] The visitors auditioned local dancers for their dance company and African Americans begin to flock to the Senegalese and Guinea classes as they had previously with the Nigerians and Ghanaians. Soon almost all African Americans involved in West African dance were performing Senegalese and Guinea dance.[4] As before, African American women were the majority participants.

Eventually, the Senegalese and Guinea visitors moved to other cities. Yet their style of dance remained popular and given their absence, African American women became the new teachers and performers of the Senegalese/Guinea dance.[5] Today, the Los Angeles West African dance community consists of approximately 200 African Americans and a small number of native Africans. This community of 200 is composed of dancers, teachers, drummers, spectators, children and dance advocates.

Current West African Dance Classes

The Dance Collective, a dance studio in Los Angeles, features Senegalese/Guinea classes taught by both native Africans and African Americans. Organized in 1992 by three African American women choreographers, the Dance Collective is located in the center of the Los Angeles African American cultural district and served as the site of my class participation and observation. Here I established the West African dance environment and demographics.

I noted that in all of the classes, women are the dancers and men are the drummers. The weekend classes are the most popular and will often have 50 or more dancers while the weekday classes will sometimes have as few as 10. African American women are the majority in all classes. Among them, there are two age groups; young women in their 20s and older women with ages ranging from 30s to 50s. In all classes, there are at least 2 or more female dancers of non-African descent in the age range of 25–30. Occasionally, there are 1–2 African American male dancers and maybe 1 male dancer of non-African descent in the age range of 30. Approximately 5–6 African American men and 2–3 native Africans play the drum accompaniment to the dance. Almost all of them are over 30.

The performance level of the dancers range from those with less than a year dance experience to professional dancer. West African dance class content includes warm-ups, practice, and performance of specific traditional dances that have been taught over and over since their introduction by the Senegalese/Guinea artists. Recently, new dances have been introduced by guest artists teaching master classes and workshops at the Dance Collective.

Womens' Roles in West African Dance

In almost all of the traditional West African dances, the women's movements emphasize physicality. For example, in the Malinke of

Guinea puberty dance, Mandiani, women are to express "energy, celebration of life and femininity" (Smith, 1991). Thus in Mandiani, one movement features women rapidly circulating their hips while simultaneously shaking their entire body and lifting up their legs in a seductive manner. In fact, Mandiani as performed by the women is such a vibrant sexual dance that often the women challenge each other to see who can "shake it the most." When a dancer is vigorously shaking her hips, her fellow dancers cheer, scream and pound the floor. If the woman is really "into it", the other women will run over to her and fan their dance skirts (lappas) behind her to suggest that she is "too hot." Drummers will also participate in this ritual by playing loudly and long so the dancer can show off.

In the dance Kakilambe, a harvesting dance of the Baga people of the Guinea forest, the Baga must appease the God Destiny who comes out every seven years after harvest time (Sendi, 1989). If the God is appeased, he will rise and bring a good harvest. To illustrate this story, women performing Kakilambe shake their torsos, shoulders and breasts to show that, indeed, they are appeasing the Destiny spirit. E-kon-kon, a harvest dance of the Jola people of Senegal and the Gambia particularly accentuates women shaking their hips. In fact, many dancers wear what is known as an "E-kon-kon belt" so that the hip-shaking will stand out. Another dance accentuating the hips is Wolo-so-don which is performed to represent the pain and suffering that African slaves endured in the Americas. This dance features both back and front thrusting of the hips while the hands are clasped together to represent shackles (Sendi, 1989).

Mandiani, Kakilambe, E-kon-kon, Wolo-so-don and other dances in the West African dance idiom demonstrate that primary roles for women in these dances is to show desirability in order to attract a mate. The women's objective is to attract a mate because a mate will lead to the ultimate aim of having a family. This portrayal of women in West African dance is consistent with the concept in many traditional West African cultures that women are not considered women until they have a husband and subsequently a family.

Comments on Women Dance Roles

I distributed a survey questionnaire to 25 African American women dancers that have been dancing for 5 or more years. Of these 25,

I randomly chose to interview 5 formally. I asked the 5 interviewees the same questions I asked in the survey questionnaires so I could seek more in-depth answers than what was written on the questionnaire form. To my surprise, I received only brief comments in both questionnaires and formal interviews, I think this is because the women believed that since I also dance, I should already know the answers.

One of the questions I asked was: Do you think there are different West African dance roles portrayed by men and women? The following are some of the comments. "The dance reflects the clearly defined roles in life of African men and women." "Roles in African life are set and so is the dance." "African dance is functional. Fertility dances are performed by women while warrior dances are performed by men." "The dance shows the work that women and men must do." "Men are masculine and they must show this; women must show that they are feminine."

The most significant question I asked focused upon what African American women think about the portrayal of women in West African dance. Comments were, "The dance shows what women can do in life"; "Women are strong, yet feminine", "Women have secondary roles." One interesting comment was that "women have positive roles in the dance because these roles are consistent with the roles in society." Another interesting comment was that the "dances tell stories and that women must act out the role that they play in the stories."

When you participate in West African dance, how do you see yourself, was also an important question. The answers I received were:" I feel myself first as a woman and then as an African." "I get great pride in my culture." "The dance role I play in class accentuates aspects of my femininity that everyday life situations neglects." "The dance allows me to feel the spirit of wholeness."

The survey respondents and interviewees were asked a total of 10 questions. The 3 questions discussed above provided me with the most information on African American women's views of their participation in West African dance. Overall, the womens' responses reveal they are aware of their roles in West African dance and believe their roles to be specific and necessary given the place that African women occupy in traditional society. None of the women, either in the formal interviews or on the questionnaires, said that the roles they play through the dance is objectionable. In fact, in light of their comments, the women all appear to enjoy emphasizing their physical desirability through West African dance. The 25 comments I received are, of course, not representative of all African American women in the West African dance community. The informants for this study, however, are experienced dancers and can be considered knowledgeable about West African dance and the community of dancers.

Gender and Culture Self-Esteem

In West African dance, one must articulate the role of either a man or woman. Otherwise they are not really dancing. This portrayal of roles in West African dance is so persuasive, that African American women gain a sense of power by dancing these roles. None of the survey respondents or interviewees actually used the word "power" in their comments, but remarks such as: "I can feel the role of a woman firstly and then as an African"; "I get a great feeling of joy and love"; "I feel like I'm Oshun {a god} or Cleopatra"; the dance accentuates aspects of my femininity", show that in the West African dance environment, African American women are transformed. This transformation gives them power and ultimately gender and cultural self-esteem. They are proud to be women and proud of their ethnic heritage.

It is obvious that the dance environment contributes as much to these feelings of gender and cultural self-esteem as the dance itself. One of the survey questions asked was "Why do you believe African American women are the majority participants in the West African dance classes?" Comments were that "dancing is feminine" and "Western culture has conditioned men to be afraid of moving their bodies". Another viewpoint was that men have no interest in dance unless they are already artists such as those in the Alvin Ailey Company or the Dance Theatre of Harlem. One woman said simply that there are just more women than men in Los Angeles. These remarks indicate that African American women view West African dance as an environment where they will be the majority. Given this environment which is composed primarily of African American women dancers, teachers, and choreograpers, allows the women freedom to assert their femininity and enhance their morale.

Conclusion

Finally, the context and the energy they have put into the dance causes African American women to consider themselves as the preservers of West African dance. West African dance is part of their culture and history and they claim it. They have developed an atmosphere in which their gender and cultural identity is clear. As a teacher and performer of West African dance, there is no doubt in my mind that West African dance provides an arena where African American womens' identity can indeed be expressed. This expression brings us affirmation of gender and cultural self.

Acknowledgements

The author would like to thank the African American women participating in the survey and formal interviews for their comments which serve as the basis for this article.

Notes

1. The definition of West African dance includes traditional dances originating from the countries of Senegal, the Gambia, Mali, Guinea, Nigeria, and Ghana.
2. Men and women of non-African descent may also gain self-esteem from West African dance. The focus in this paper, however, is to demonstrate the connections between West African dance, and culture and gender identity for African American women.
3. The same situation took place in New York and other urban areas when Senegalese and Guinea artists visited. African Americans were fascinated by the dance and the Djimbe drum.
4. African Americans continued to participate in Nigerian and Ghanaian dance, but not with the same fervor as in the 1960s.
5. Throughout the rest of the paper, Senegalese and Guinea dance will be referred to as a unit, Senegalese/Guinea. Although the dances of these two countries differ, they are often performed together in the West African dance community.

References

Long, Richard. (1989) *The Black tradition in American dance.* New York: Rizzoli International Publications, Inc.
Sendi, Takiyah. (1989) *Information on West African dances* (leaflet). Los Angeles, California.
Smith, Phylisé. (1991) *Los Angeles African Americans: Expressions of cultural identity through participation in West African dance.* (Master's Thesis) University of California Los Angeles: Department of Dance.

Choreography and Dance
1998, Vol. 5, Part 1, pp. 79–86
Photocopying permitted by license only

"Woman," Women, and Subversion: Some Nagging Questions from a Dance Historian

Ann Daly

Daly considers the ways that gender-based research has challenged how dance history is defined, theorized, and written. More than a decade after the introduction of the "male gaze" theory to dance history, Daly calls for a renewed interrogation of feminist theory, in order to continue generating new sets of questions and new stories for dance history. She outlines two areas of inquiry. The first is the development of a productive model of cultural change that acknowledges the agency of women. The second is a critique of the gender politics of logocentric cultural theory. Borrowing from the work of Pierre Bourdieu, Daly suggests an analytical framework for opening up new inroads in the history of women in dance. Finally, she advocates for an intellectual flexibility in the development of a feminist approach to dance history.

KEY WORDS   Facts, discourse, cultural change, dance history.

Today I will focus specifically on questions, rather than answers, for two reasons. One, because I am at a place right now in my own research, between projects, where I am involved more with questions than with answers. Second, because I do believe that, in the long run, questions are more important than answers. For new knowledge or new ways of looking and understanding will never be produced if the same old questions keep getting asked. As Albert Einstein (Einstein and Leopold, 1938) wrote, "The formulation of a problem is often more essential than its solution, which may be merely a matter of mathematical or experimental skill. To raise new questions, new possibilities, to regard old questions from a new angle, requires creative imagination and marks real advances in science."[1]

Addressed from a specifically feminist perspective, the gender issues that entered the discourse of dance history in the late 1980s encouraged us to ask new questions. The kinds of nagging questions that reframe the very field itself. Nagging questions that we recognize as the way that children make sense of the world in the first place. Questions like "what if?," "how come?," "who says?," or, the perennial favorite of any creative soul, "why not?"

Inserting the question of gender into dance history also broke open the issues of truth and authority. It demonstrated that history can, and should, be written and re-written and re-written again. Different stories will be told, depending upon what questions are asked. No one story inherently holds truth and authority, and the basis upon which we evaluate the relative merit of one story over another is not the mere accumulation of facts. "Facts" are not at all the protagonists of dance history. They certainly are necessary, but they are not sufficient, for facts mean nothing until they are interpreted. Facts are highly unstable. They must be choreographed, given particular shape through the questions that are asked, the person doing the asking, and the context in which they are placed. Edwin Denby (1965) made the point eloquently:

> About facts, too, what interests me just now is how differently they can look, one sees them one way and one sees them another way another time, and yet one is still seeing the same fact. Facts have a way of dancing about, now performing a solo then reappearing in the chorus, linking themselves now with facts of one kind, now with facts of another, and quite changing their style as they do. Of course you have to know the facts so you can recognize them, or you can't appreciate how they move, how they keep dancing.

Gender-based research in dance history succeeded in breaking open a whole new way of looking at old, so-called "facts." It has given us new eyes through which to tell more stories, and different stories.

When I began engaging feminist theory as a tool for looking at historical dance practices, some 10 years ago, the questions focused on the mechanisms of representation of Woman. The theory of the "male gaze" was tremendously powerful, because it explained so much about the way that women had been positioned in dance and, indeed, in all the arts (see Daly, 1991). The theory prompted us to ask questions that had never been asked before. Like all paradigm shifts, it at first seemed to explain everything. And, like all paradigm shifts, after the first flush of discovery, its weaknesses began to appear. Feminist theory has been around long enough now that it needs to be renewed. I want to call for an interrogation of feminist theory with its own unflinching eye, so that we can continue to come up with new sets of questions, and new stories.

The emphasis here, I should make clear, is not on the new just for the sake of novelty. When I advocate the asking of new questions and the telling of new stories, I mean to communicate the importance of producing a deeper, a broader, and a more complex discourse. I use the word "discourse" instead of the term "dance history" because I want to frame and define our field not as a fixed thing, like a puzzle in which a "fact," once set in its place, is finished and fixed forever, but as an ongoing dialogue—no, a polylogue—in which the facts or stories are never fixed, because the big picture is always in process, always dancing.

* * *

There are two questions in particular that have been nagging at me during the past year. Each one—the first about developing a productive model of cultural change that acknowledges the agency of women and the second about critiquing the gender politics of logocentrism—is crystallized in recent personal encounters.

* * *

The first encounter took place at the joint conference of the Congress On Research in Dance and the Society of Dance History Scholars, which took place last summer in New York City. The conference concentrated on American dance of the 1930s, a rather neglected period. What an epiphany the gala concert was for me, as I watched reconstructions of dances by members of the New Dance Group. It was a whole new world of visionary dances, most of them by women, that intrigued and exhilarated me. I remember listening to Doris Hering interview Sophie Maslow and Jane Dudley. Strong and generous and no-nonsense, these women recalled a life of tough but committed decisions, in less-than-easy circumstances. I felt great respect and affection for them, and it disconcerted me that some feminist theoretical models would see only that they had failed to overthrow patriarchy single-handedly. This experience intensified my discomfort with a theory of identity and subjectivity that denies women any agency and cannot conceive of culture as potentially productive as well as inherently reproductive. The question nagged at me: Can't I find or construct a theory of cultural change that allows for women as potentially productive agents rather than as reproductive ciphers? Must I have to choose among equally unsatisfying frameworks: one that denies women the agency that men possess (e.g., the theory of the "male gaze"); one that denies everyone agency (e.g., Foucault), and one, the default model, that denies any cultural impediment to agency (e.g., the American Dream)?

During the years I spent researching Isadora Duncan, I came to realize that real women, as historical subjects rather than as cultural constructs called "Woman," engage in aesthetic practices that are complexly matrixed and many-layered. It is fruitless to ask whether her dancing was a subversion or reinforcement of the status quo, because in some ways it was a subversion, and in some ways it was a reinforcement. Duncan exploited certain dominant discourses, such as class distinction and nativistic nationalism, to propagate other, more oppositional discourses, such as female autonomy. And these discourses and their interrelationships never remained static (see Daly, 1995).

As a way out of this impasse, I have been reading the work of French anthropologist/sociologist Pierre Bourdieu (1984, 1990). Bourdieu conceives of society as being organized into "fields," each of which is a structured and structuring system of social relations with its own logic. Any field, including that of Culture, has its own economy, so to speak, in which capital—economic, social, educational, symbolic—must be accumulated in order to advance or dominate in that particular field. The strategies for accumulating such capital and for gaining legitimacy, or distinction, are regulated by the field itself. These predisposed strategies, a generative constellation of tacit, internalized, embodied principles and practices, are what Bourdieu calls a field's "habitus." These unwritten rules are learned not explicitly, but implicitly, through practice in the field. Although the general contours of the habitus are shared by each player in the field, each individual, having come from a different background and thus occupying a different position within the field, has a slightly different "habitus." Cultural belief, Bourdieu argues, is not in our heads, but in our bodies, what he calls the bodily "hexis."

The usefulness of Bourdieu's scheme to a gender-based dance history is its attention to the ways an artist constructs difference and distinction, in practice and in the reception of that practice.

Adapting Bourdieu's model, we can look at how women choreographers have made specific choices in pre-existing, intersecting fields: how women strategically deployed economic, social, intellectual, as well as cultural institutions and practices (see Daly, 1994).

For the study of dance history as social practice (rather than just aesthetic object), Bourdieu offers a theoretical and analytical framework which offers a plausible alternative to the two extremes of cultural interpretation: on the one hand, subjectivism, which attributes behavior solely to the agency of the individual, and on the other hand, objectivism, which attributes behavior to the rules of social structure. It offers us a way to see that women choreographers and dancers are neither "geniuses," forging new practices out of thin air, nor passive functions of their cultural contexts. Yes, a woman's choices and strategies are delimited by the institutions and practices of her day, but choices are made, nonetheless. Bourdieu's concept of the "habitus" yokes together internal choice and external conditions into a mutually conditional and—this is most important—*generative* dynamic. He posits the social agent as occupying a relational, potentially changeable position in an equally changeable field. Thus we can recognize the social structures and practices through which a woman negotiated her art while also acknowledging her agency. And vice versa. We can recognize her agency and still recognize the social structures which gave rise to the conditions of that agency. The feminist historical project is not simply about divining a woman's "intention," but about teasing apart her actual choices in relation to her possible choices. It is not about determining whether or not she lives up to current theoretical models, which seems fundamentally to disrespect women in a decidedly un-feminist way. We may critique her choices, but we need to recognize and acknowledge that choices were indeed made.

As feminist historians, we need to recognize both the limits and possibilities that constituted a woman's "habitus." We need to take into account social limits and possibilities: the limits and possibilities of education, of money, of class, of race and ethnicity, of the body, of sexuality, of particular artistic genres. Just as important, we need to take into account the limits and possibilities of our own conditions and knowledge.

These days, it is impossible for me to read gender without reading its connection to race, class, and sexuality. By theorizing the interaction of various fields of social life, Bourdieu suggests the complexity of artistic practice. I am looking for a more complex understanding and analysis of how culture operates in constructing the gendered dancing body. I would like to expand the borders of the social context in which we make sense of women's artistry. I would like to take into consideration the meaning of patronage, performance venues, marketing, body techniques, and schools, as well as religious background, economic status, and social contacts.

* * *

The second encounter took place not even a month ago, and it pulled to shore, so to speak, an issue that has been lapping at the edges of my work for some time now. I was attending a women's studies seminar at the University of Texas, where a visiting scholar had presented a fascinating paper on the dance craze in the 1910s in Australia. One of the questions posed to the visiting scholar went something like this: "It's interesting what happens when women have only their bodies with which to speak. In this time and place, why dance? In other words, why was it dance through which they communicated?" I had been quiet up until now, preferring to listen. But I could hardly remain silent any longer. To this question, "Why dance," I rather abruptly replied, "Why NOT dance?" I went on to suggest that women—and men, for that matter—are ALWAYS "speaking" with and through their bodies. Furthermore, I challenged the assumption that nonverbal communication is inferior and somehow less authentic or valid than verbal communication. Of course, the idea of the body as the essential realm of "Woman" is the larger context here. This idea has served to marginalize women, bodies, and dance, so it is a notion that we tend to reject, but in doing so, we are also rejecting the whole of nonverbal communication, and, by extension, dance itself. The question I have been asking in this regard has to do with the politics of logocentrism, and the resulting quandary for women in general and dance scholars in particular, who do not want to reject the nonverbal but, at the same time, do not want their involvement with the non-verbal to be read as "feminine" and therefore marginalized. It's not only a question about the status of dance in culture and its potential for producing change but also a question about the status of dance history and dance historians within the academy.

For all the volume of current writing on the "body," inspired largely by the groundbreaking work of theorists such as Foucault, Bakhtin, and the French school of *l'ecriture feminine*, the body is still approached as the suspect "other." The body is still posited as a presence, in a deconstructive moment that privileges absence. The body, when it is taken into account, is treated, more often than not, as an inscriptive surface, a pre-text for language. And the body, when its bodily practices are directly addressed, is treated, more often than not, as a means of cultural reproduction, rather than a means of cultural change.

In addition, many current theories of identity, subjectivity, language, and culture are rooted in Lacanian psychoanalysis, which constructs subjectivity and culture as the very break from an infantile (nonverbal) plenitude of the body into the world of (verbal) language. Within this model, nonverbal practices are relegated to the realm of the asocial, the maternal, the hysteric; obviously, then, within this model, nonverbal practices cannot produce cultural change. And, for women, alignment with nonverbal practices serves only to reinforce their marginality. This doesn't leave much work for the scholar studying dance as cultural production, and especially for the scholar studying dance as a feminist practice.

So, as that scholar, I ask: What would result from a re-reading of cultural theory that does not repress the body as "pre-verbal"; that does not marginalize dance as "non-verbal" and "feminine"; that, avoiding the privileging of either of the terms "verbal" or "nonverbal," underscores the dialectic between the two? The nature of this dialectic, I suggest, is a fundamental issue underlying any cultural theory of dance, including a gender-based cultural theory of dance.

I have been looking in four places for clues in dealing with the feminist implications of this dialectic: French theorist Julia Kristeva's *Revolution in Poetic Language*; psychoanalyst Daniel Stern's *The Interpersonal World of the Infant*; philosopher Mark Johnson's *The Body in the Mind: The Bodily Basis of Meaning, Imagination, and Reason*; and philosopher Drew Leder's *The Absent Body*. I have found these works useful for questioning the privilege given to verbal language, and its alignment with the "masculine" in our culture. By deconstructing the opposition between the verbal and the nonverbal in many of our cultural theories, we can make a space for dance, and especially that of women, as a potentially productive cultural practice.

* * *

To borrow a longstanding phrase from feminist literary critic Annette Kolodny (1980), I would like to advocate for a "playful pluralism" in our discipline's gender-based research. The goal is to accept all points of view but subject them all to fair and fundamental scrutiny. This principle of simultaneous acceptance and scrutiny captures our challenge as dance historians: to respect differences while remaining intellectually engaged. No one theory or framework or approach is appropriate for all objects of study or for all researchers and the questions they choose to ask. Only intellectual flexibility will enable us to broaden, deepen, and enrich the field of dance history. There are many women to write about, many questions to ask, and many stories to tell. Women's lives in dance are not reducible to a formula, and it is only appropriate to the spirit of a feminist project to respect and even encourage difference as the very condition of both change and knowledge.

Notes

1. As a keynote address, this paper was written specifically for oral delivery. Rather than re-write the paper, I have chosen to retain its original style.

References

Bourdieu, P. (1984) *Distinction: A Social Critique of the Judgement of Taste*, translated by Richard Nice. Cambridge: Harvard University Press.

Bourdieu, P. (1990) *The Logic of Practice*, translated by Richard Nice. Stanford: Stanford University Press.

Daly, A. (1994) Isadora Duncan and the distinction of dance. In *American Studies Journal*, **35**(1), 5–23.

——. (1995) *Done into Dance: Isadora Duncan in America*. Bloomington: Indiana University Press.

——. (1991) An unlimited partnership: dance and feminist analysis. *Dance Research Journal*, **23**(1), 2–5.

Denby, E. (1965) Dancers, buildings and people in the streets. In *Dancers, Buildings and People in the Streets*, pp. 171–180. New York: Popular Library.

Einstein, A. and L. Infeld. (1938) *The Evolution of Physics*. p. 95. New York: Simon and Schuster.

Johnson, M. (1987) *The Body in the Mind*. Chicago: University of Chicago Press.

Kolodny, A. (1980) Dancing through the minefield: some observations on the theory, practice, and politics of a feminist literary criticism. *Feminist Studies*, **6**(1), 1–25.

Kristeva, J. (1984) *Revolution in Poetic Language*, translated by Margaret Waller. New York: Columbia University Press.

Leder, D. (1990) *The Absent Body*. Chicago: University of Chicago Press.

Stern, D. (1985) *The Interpersonal World of the Infant*. New York: Basic Books, Inc.

Choreography and Dance
1998, Vol. 5, Part 1, pp. 87–102
Photocopying permitted by license only

Dance Education and Gender in Japan

Michie Hayashi

In 1994, dance became coeducational in junior and senior high schools in Japan, an educational dance innovation. After the 19th century, the Japanese government imported a European educational system containing physical education and dance. Females were taught dance; males were not. Males were mainly taught martial arts and European gymnastics; females were taught European rhythmic dance. With the exception of Japanese traditional dance, for example Noh and Kabuki which were exclusively male, dance was predominantly female. The general public began to think of it as a part of the female character. Dancing was considered desirable and valuable for females but worthless, strange and abnormal for males. The reasons why men in Japan do not dance nor have the desire to become involved in dance are outlined in the following sections: (1) dance education and its cultural background; (2) the development of dance education and physical education; (3) the meaning of the coeducation in dance, its changing views and problems.

KEY WORDS Physical education, martial arts, European gymnastics, European rhythmic dance, Noh, Kabuki, female character, coeducation in dance.

Introduction

In 1994, under the new teaching guideline as set out by the Education Ministry, dance became coeducational in junior and senior high schools. This represents a revolution in how dance education is viewed in Japan because it is the first time that male students can study dance since the modern educational system was established in the 1870s. For about 130 years, male students never had the chance to study dance in school, even if they wanted to. Gradually males were excluded from dance itself and even the appreciation of dance works. As a result, today men and women do not have a dance culture in common and do not communicate through dance.

Figure 12   Noh. Photo: unknown.

Because Japanese men danced before the Meiji era, these phenomena are not a true condition for Japanese people. I propose that these gender roles were influenced by political systems, and in particular, the educational system.

The purpose of this paper is to explore: (1) dance education and its cultural background; (2) the development of dance and physical education; and (3) the meaning of coeducation in dance, its changing views and problems.

Dance Education and its Cultural Background

Traditional Japanese styles of dance, such as Noh and Kabuki, have never been taught in the public school system under the modern educational system. After the isolationist policy of the Edo era (1603–1867), the Meiji government essentially imported an educational system, based upon the philosophy and methods of European models of physical education. In order to build a prosperous nation and create a strong army which would rank with European countries, males and females were educated separately, with different objectives and methods (Matsumoto, 1992, pp. 52–69).

Rather than learning traditional Japanese dance, males were mainly taught martial arts (Kendo and Judo), European gymnastics, and sports, in order to foster strong soldiers and workers. Females were mainly taught European rhythmic and folk dance to make women "feminine" and to encourage them to support a patriarchal structure in society. Gradually a fixed view of gender was established through these educational experiences. Males had to be strong and females had to be beautiful, elegant, and graceful. It is not an overstatement to say that dances were utilized by the government as an instrument in establishing an ideal female image. Correspondingly, dance was excluded from male education in order to build a strong male image. This was a new phenomenon because previously females had not been allowed to perform Japanese traditional dances. To further explain this phenomenon, we need to consider why, historically, only males were allowed to perform traditional Japanese dance.

Historically, dance was an important part of and the method of communication with god and nature without the distinction of gender. Later, with the establishment of a political system in which men administered the affairs of politics, dance was performed exclusively by men. In fact, dance was the most extravagant entertainment that

Figure 13   Kabuki. Photo: unknown.

men of power possessed, and Noh, Kabuki, and other Japanese traditional dances were performed only by males. These dances were supported by a hereditary system, that is, they were handed down from father to son as a profession of the family (Gunji, 1971, pp. 60–62). The male performers of Japanese traditional dances were confined to private sects. Each taught its own method or style of movement and passed it down through the generations.

Kabuki was originally created by a woman named "Okuni" (Gunji, 1971, p. 81). She was artistically fascinating and attractive. She impressed the audience greatly, but dances performed by women were disparaged by men because the men connected dance with money and immoral sexual behavior. Finally in October 1629, the government forbade "Female kabuki" because it was thought to contribute to a perceived deterioration of society (Nagatake, 1993, p. 93). After this decree, for about 250 years, females were not allowed to dance in public. This lasted until approximately the beginning of the Meiji era, when women were again accepted into the dance world as a result of the congruence of their strong desire to dance, and the government's desire to attract the public to theaters in order to increase sales in shops in the surrounding areas (Endo, 1993, p. 145). One example of this is the "Miyako Odori"[1] which was performed by women in Kyoto. While it was thought to be a symbol of women's revolution, actually it had a political and economic purpose, since, at that time, political leaders considered women as commodities. Even though the government exploited their desire to dance, irrespective of the reason, women finally had the chance to dance in public. Parallel with this permission for women to dance in society in 1872, dance was introduced as a part of physical education in schools for females but not for males.

An important function of the educational system is to teach the meanings of traditional culture from one generation to the next. Ironically, the Japanese government did not include Japanese traditional dance in the educational system. If the Meiji government had included it in the curriculum, males might not have been excluded from dance as they presently are. One reason for Japanese traditional dance's not having been taught in schools was explained in a theory by Mr. Takechi (1985, pp. 272–276), a famous director and critic. He wrote that the Meiji government placed an emphasis upon changing body movement and behavioral patterns of young men. Thus, in order to attain the objective of a strong national army, the government taught movement to young men and women differently.

Figure 14   Miyako Odori. Photo: unknown.

Originally, the Japanese people were a farming culture. Their movement pattern while working was referred to as "namba" (Takechi, 1985, p. 221). People walked forward, the arm and leg of the same side moving concurrently, with the center of gravity low in their bodies. They kept their knees bent and shuffled their feet along the ground. This "namba" figure couldn't create centrifugal force; it couldn't run fast, turn, or jump. In order to run fast and jump lightly, a new kind of movement training was needed. The center of gravity had to be kept higher in the body by bending the knees while lifting up the thighs. This type of training was introduced as part of the education for young males who were eager to learn and contribute to their nation. Through this method of physical education which incorporates gymnastics and martial arts, male students were trained to make their bodies functional, efficient, and strong.

The Development of Dance Education and Physical Education

To discuss dance education in Japan, one needs to understand it's relationship to the physical education system.

Although the educational system, established by the Meiji government in 1872, included physical education for the first time, a consistent and permanent method of education was not yet determined. At first, this physical education consisted mainly of gymnastics, sports, and martial arts for men, dance and gymnastics for women. Men and women were separately educated in physical education as well as all other subjects. Before the Meiji era women were not educated at all, but the modern educational system stressed equal opportunity for men and women with educational liberty for women, under the law.

After 1872, some girls' high schools were constructed. In response to an increasing number of female students, the government gradually built up objectives and a curriculum which intended to foster the ideal image of women. In 1878, the government invited G.E. Lieland, an American gymnastic teacher to teach students of the Tokyo Normal School for Women (Kawamura, 1972, p. 140). From the end of 1800s to the beginning of 1900s, the government dispatched some female teachers of physical education to study abroad, in the U.S.A. and Europe, in order to research physical education methods for women, mainly the basic techniques of western dance. Physical

Figure 15   Female Dancing as Taught in Schools. Photo: unknown.

education was strengthened by including western aesthetic dance, gymnastic dance, folk dance, and some sports. As a consequence, until about 1935, many philosophies, theories, and practical methods of female physical education were imported from the U.S.A. and Europe. Based on that information, original Japanese methods of women's physical education were gradually established. At the beginning of 1900, gymnastic, folk, and aesthetic dance performed by women were admired as the essence of athletic meetings (Matsumoto, 1992, pp. 52–69). Through these processes, female students were being educated to have beautiful dispositions and graceful behavior.

As explained above, in Japan the Ministry of Education has strictly controlled school curricula from the beginning of the Meiji era and dance was only included in physical education for women. Dance has not been taught to male students for about 120 years. Beginning in about 1930, Japan was at war, and the government utilized physical education programs to train its citizens for war time. Since the government aimed to train women to endure the hardships of wartime, dance was not a priority. Although dance was still included in physical education, it needed to be taught according to this new objective. Dance educators struggled with their own views of the purpose of dance as opposed to the requests of the government; the existence of dance education was threatened.

After World War II, creative dance with a strong American influence was introduced to the Japanese educational system stressing individuality, originality, and creativity (Kataoka, 1992, pp. 119–121). In the U.S.A., "during the late 1950s and early 1960s, the leaders of dance educators pressed even more strongly for the recognition of dance as an area separate from physical education, and one which was essentially an art form" (Kraus, 1969, p. 262). The Japanese Society of Physical Education held repeated symposiums dealing with the problems of dance and physical education from 1964 to 1967, but the discussion of whether dance is an art or physical education has continued. Japanese dance educators are in a dilemma. Although the objectives of dance education and physical education are very different, dance is still very much a part of physical education.

Since dance was taught by women solely a "dance equals women"[2] theory was established. As a result, during the twentieth century, except for traditional dances which were still performed by men, dance in Japan became predominantly female (Umesao, 1988,

p. 212). The general public began to think that dance was part of the female character, that dancing was desirable and valuable for females but worthless, strange, and abnormal for males. These points of view towards dance gradually sank into the Japanese consciousness, and a prejudice against male dancing was created. In the U.S.A. during the 1960s, "in a number of situations, teachers have been successful in involving boys in modern dance activities. At Washington Park High School, an all boys modern dance club composed of members of school's athletic teams, gave impressive performances." (Kraus, 1969, p. 288).

Beginning with the period after World War II, the Ministry of Education changed the curriculum every ten years according to the changes in society. Some researchers and critics described the positive effects of dance education on both male and female students. The essence of dance was described as an activity that is connected to human life giving positive and pleasant feelings to any performer, whether male or female. Just as in music and other art forms, body movement is an expression of inner feelings, so dance is valuable for all people regardless of gender or age (Matsumoto, 1980, p. 9). Despite these emerging views, dance continued to be closed to male students even to those who wanted it. It is because of the influence of a long history of education that men don't recognize the value of dance. In old times both males and females had danced according to their desire to dance; however, the modern educational system stressed forming separate roles of gender through "dance education". In other countries traditional dances are included in the curriculum; however, dance education in Japan is peculiar because it totally excluded tradition and focused on imported dances only (Kunieda, 1989). Modernization of Japan caused a dramatic change in the dance world. Men, who formerly glorified dance, disappeared from the dance world; conversely, women, who had once been excluded, advanced into the dance world.

Since 1988, the All Japan Dance Festival-Kobe has been held for university and high school students. Men can enter both the competitive section and attendance section (Figure 1). As evidenced by Figure 16, very few male university students and few or no male high school students chose to participate, showing how great an influence the idea of gender specific dance education has had. Still today almost all dance teachers are females. Even though the teachers may not have been specifically educated in dance, they still

Year	University	High school	Total
Competitive Section			
1989	547(29)	750(8)	1297(37)
1990	700(36)	923(2)	1623(38)
1991	766(55)	1031(0)	1797(55)
1992	824(78)	1072(2)	1896(80)
1993	768(62)	987(0)	1755(62)
1994	829(87)	941(5)	1770(92)
Attendance Section			
1989	405(15)	409(21)	814(36)
1990	431(49)	294(4)	725(53)
1991	438(32)	505(0)	943(32)
1992	524(55)	519(3)	1043(58)
1993	450(41)	592(6)	1042(47)
1994	631(60)	615(4)	1246(64)

(from the report of ADF-Kobe Executive Committee)

Figure 16   The number of high school and university participants for the All Japan Dance Festival—Kobe from 1989–1994. The number of male participants is indicated in parentheses.

must teach dance simply because they are female. While in the Meiji era women could elect to dance, it has now became an obligation for women in physical education, regardless of their desire.

People had never questioned the previous educational philosophy of only having females participate in dance; the system was accepted without understanding the reasons for it. We might have been under the illusion that dancing originated from the biological character of women (Umesao, 1988, pp. 212–213); that women were naturally attracted to dance and men were not, but in fact this attitude was created and promoted by the educational system. In 1994, however, under the new educational system, for the first time in history, dance became coeducational in junior and senior high schools (Education Ministry, 1990). Now there seems to be a general understanding that dance education in Japan must be considered an important subject for both genders. Dance education for both genders has finally started in Japan!

The Meaning of the Coeducation in Dance:
Its Changing Views and Problems

The theory that the ability to dance is a female characteristic is disproved when we look back upon the history of dance in Japan. Perhaps the relationships between dance and gender are the hidden reason why men do not dance.

In Europe, in the 19th century, the industrial revolution took dance away from young men (Fonteyn, 1979, p. 77). As a result men vanished from the dance world, including the ballet world. Sports and gymnastics replaced dance as physical culture. In the Christian cultural sphere, where modern sports were born and developed, sports were played by men under a patriarchal ideology (Esashi, 1992, p. 21), and sports sexism was developed. Men were prohibited to dance, thus social prejudice was born. When the Japanese government imported the educational system from Europe, they also imported a value system in which men played sports and women danced. These values fit very well into the Japanese government's way of thinking. Sports were aggressive, offensive, and positive, so they were appropriated by the government with the intention to educate young men as strong soldiers and good workers. This government-sponsored ideology was stressed in schools, and dance was not considered appropriate for making strong men. Through education, some "myths" about dance and men were gradually created. These "myths" controlled people's minds through emotion rather than logic (Hasegawa, 1992, pp. 56–57). Before this education system was imported, the "myth" was that dance was immoral for women, but acceptable for men.

The following "myths" could explain why males were excluded from dance: dance makes men feminine; dance is not appropriate for a strong male body; males have an inferiority complex and do not have the desire to become involved in dance (Hayashi, 1996). Just as the myth that it is unacceptable for women to participate in sports activities is collapsing (Saeki, 1984), the myths that men do not dance is also gradually disappearing. Women are advancing in sports, as men are returning to the dance world. Thus there is evidence that the former government restrictions aimed at creating an ideal image of gender are collapsing.

In an industrialized society, gender differences tend to expand, while in an information society they tend to contract (Umesao, 1988, p. 213). As Japan is becoming an information society, dance

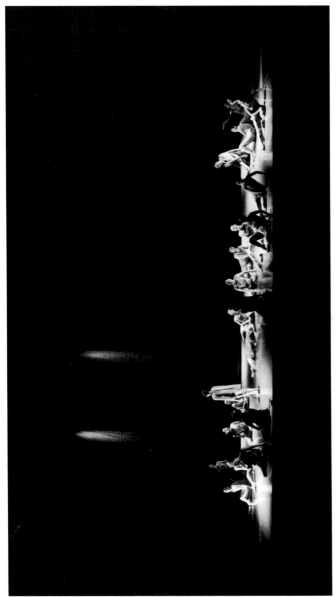

Figure 17 Dream. Osaka University of Health and Sport Sciences dance club. Photo: Osaka University.

sexism is disappearing. One example of such a change started about 15 years ago when young Japanese boys and girls began to dance in groups in parks and on streets around the country, especially in big cities such as Tokyo and Osaka. Young people are using their bodies for self expression. This new phenomenon began with the adventurous behavior and curiosity of young people (Kawai, 1989, p. 253), and it is seen as an indication that the world of dance in Japan is changing.

Dancing is a form of self expression. Just as it is natural for humans to desire to move or play sports, it is also natural for them to desire to jump for joy or stamp their feet in anger (Matsumoto, 1980, p. 9). To reflect this understanding, playing sports should not be just the privilege of men, nor should dancing be for women only in the education system.

There are, however, currently some problems with dance education. The older generation of male physical education teachers still have rather fixed gender role attitudes. Generally, they disagree with coeducation in dance (Arima, 1996). In contrast, the younger generation of teachers have more flexible gender role attitudes and favor coeducational dance. A 1996 survey asking the opinions of male and female teachers concerning coeducational dance shows the current difficulties and limitations. About 60% of male physical education teachers in their late 30s are still opposed to coeducation (Arima, 1996, p. 28). It may take some time for men and women to be completely equal, but in the future it is possible men and women will cooperate in teaching young students, just as they are doing in teaching sports.

Coeducational dance has come about as a result of changing points of view toward gender in Japanese society. Dance education in Japan has just started under a new theory; therefore, methods of coeducation, especially concerning dance and male students, need to be discussed. If coeducation is successful, men and women can have the same understanding and both genders can naturally communicate with each other through dance. Dance will truly become an art in which both genders cooperate. This can become a reality through dance education.

Summary

Before the Meiji era, Japanese traditional dances were performed and supported by males, but consequently males were excluded from dance because of the influence of education. The Meiji government had to catch up with European countries in order to rival their development, so Japan imported an educational system from the West. The government educated males and females separately with different objectives. Males were taught to be strong and to contribute to the army, while females were taught to be beautiful and womanly and to support males. Dance was utilized as an instrument only in the education of females. Thus during the past 120 years, the prejudice that dance was worthless and abnormal for males was created and sustained through education.

In 1994, dance became coeducational in junior and senior high schools. Dance education began to reflect changing attitudes in Japanese society. When gender ideals are separated from political domination, the prejudice toward dance will vanish. Japanese have a recent history in which the government stressed gender differences in education, especially physical education and dance.

It is the now the goal of educators to teach dance to all young people regardless of gender. Through education, prejudices towards dance will vanish and dance will become an area in which both men and women participate.

Notes

1. Miyako Odori is a spring dance festival in the old capital of Kyoto. It was created by Haruko Katayama who was a great dancer of traditional Kyoto Dance. After the capital was moved to Tokyo, the politicians planned to hold an exposition in order to revive old Kyoto; Miyako Odori was in celebration of it. In April of every year, Geiko and Maiko dance in Gion. Geiko are known as Geisha in many other parts of Japan; however, Geiko are specific to the Kyoto area. Geiko are highly proficient in all Japanese arts: dancing, singing, playing traditional instruments, storytelling, and tea ceremony. Maiko are young apprentices of Geiko.
2. Dance belongs to women. The word "Dance" directly implies women, and "women" directly implies dance. Particularly in schools, dance is left to female teachers.

References

Arima, F. (1996) *The Attitude toward the Co-education of Dance of Physical Education Teacher—Focusing on Gender*, unpublished Master Thesis of Osaka University of Health and Sport Sciences.

Esashi, S. (1992) *Josei Supotsu no Shakaigaku* (Sociology of Women's Sports) Tokyo: Fumaidoshuppan.

Endo, K. (1993) *Sansei Inoue Yachiyo* (Third generation of the Inoue Yachiyo School of Dance). Tokyo: Ribropoto.

Fonteyne, M. (1979) *The Magic of Dance* (Dansu no Miryoku. translated by Yukawa, K.). Tokyo: Sinshokan.

Gunji, M. (1971) *Odori no Bigaku* (Esthetics of Japanese Dance). Tokyo: Engekishuppansha.

Hasegawa, K. (1992) *Jenda no Shakaigaku* (The Sociology of Gender) Tokyo: Sinyosha.

Hayashi, M. (1996) Buyo Bunka no Kyoyu—Dansukyoiku ni Dansei no Siten wo (Dance as a Joint Property of Male and Female—The Necessity of Male's Point of View to Dance Education). *Taiku no Kagaku.* **46**(3), 237–240.

Kataoka, Y. (1991) *Buyogaku Kogi* (Dance and Dance Education). Tokyo: Taishukan Shoten.

Kawai, M. (1989) *Gakumon no Boken* (An Adventure of Learning) Tokyo: Koseishuppansha.

Kawamura, H. (1972) *Nihon Taiikusi.* (Japanese History of Physical Education). Tokyo: Shoyoshoin.

Kraus, R. (1969) *History of the Dance, in Art and Education.* New Jersey: Prentice-hall, Inc.

Kunieda, T. (1989) Showasi ni okeru Dansukyoiku (The History of Dance Education in Showa Era) *Taiikuka Kyoiku* **37**(10), 38–42.

Matsumoto, C. (1992) *Dansu no Kyoikugaku* (Pedagogy of Dance). Tokyo: Tokumashoten.

——. (1980) *Dansu, Hyogen, Gakushu Shido Zensho* (Teaching Methods of Dance and Expression for Elementary School and High School). Tokyo; Taishuukan Shoten.

Ministry of Education, (1990) *Gakushu Sido Yoryo* (Teaching Guideline). Tokyo: Higashiyama Shobo.

Nagatake, Y. (1993) *Opera to Kabuki* (Opera and Kabuki). Tokyo: Maruzen.

Saeki, T. (1984) Josei Supotsu no Gendaiteki Kadai (Modern Subjects of Female Sports). *Josi Taiiku*, **26**(8), 2–6.

Takechi, T. (1985) *Buyo no Gei* (The Art of Dance). Tokyo: Tokyo Shoseki.

Umesao, T. (1988) *Onna to Bunmei* (Women and Civilization). Tokyo: Chuo Koronsha.

Yamazumi, M. (1990) *Nihon Kyoiku Shosi* (The Japanese History of Education). Tokyo: Iwanami Shoten.

Every effort has been made to trace the ownership of all copyrighted material in this article. In event of any questions about the use of any material, the author, while expressing regret for any inadvertent error, will be happy to make the necessary acknowledgment in future printings.

Choreography and Dance
1998, Vol. 5, Part 1, pp. 103–115
Photocopying permitted by license only

Body and Identity in Afro-Brazilian Candomblé

Eva Zorrilla Tessler

Candomblé is one among many African derived religions practiced today in Brazil. For Candomblé the human body becomes the crossroads between the sacred and the profane through the phenomenon of trance (triggered by dance and music). This paper examines trance within the initiation process and suggests a connection between Candomblé's use of the body in performance and alternative constructions of peoples' identities *vis-à-vis* the Brazilian state. The Brazilian state historically has established the body as a commodity or as a machine. Identity is a performance accomplishment compelled in many respects by dominant ways of living and thinking (hegemony); at the same time, identity is transformational, challenging hegemonic practices, meanings, and values through performance. Such construction of identities, and the resulting empowerment it provides, originate in the training of the human body for trance/performance which contradicts the views of the body as a commodity and as a machine.

KEY WORDS   Body in trance, identity, Orixá, Candomblé, Brazil, State.

Leticia Just Says "No" to Valium

"Odo-iya-é" cried Pai Saponan de Omolú and everybody else in the room answered "odo-iya-é, Iemanjá". Cida, the Little Mother shook a little bell (**adjá**) furiously. From the next room, through a door covered with a curtain of beads, appeared the imposing **Orixá Iemanjá** in the quality of **Inaé**, the goddess of the Ocean and mother of the Orixás, dressed sumptuously in blue and white. She carried a fan and a short sword. The people in the big room (**barracão**) which was profusely adorned with flowers, stopped dancing and reverently touched the dirt floor. The three musicians started to play their drums, the crowd began to sing and Iemanjá slowly initiated a dance, her arms

103

suggesting the movement of the waves. People offered her bottles
of perfume and flowers. At times, Iemanjá moved with a vibratory
quality which provoked trance in other people. An elderly woman
began to shake, folded her arms and legs into her torso and fell on
the floor. Other women picked her up and carried her inside. No
one was supposed to fall into trance in this particular ceremony
except for the woman who personified Iemanjá. Her name is Leticia
and this was her **Saida de Iaô**, the culminating ceremony of her
Candomblé initiation.

After dancing and receiving offerings Leticia/Iemanjá sat on a
chair and presided over the rest of the ceremony which lasted all
night. By 5 a.m., the smell of rotten flowers became overwhelming,
the drumming unbearable, the circular pattern of the dancers, men
and women dressed in white, overpowering and my companion
and I had to step outside. In the tiny patio some people were sleeping on the ground next to the coagulated blood of the sacrified
animals (goats, chickens and ducks), the ritual food for Iemanjá.
Shortly before dawn, several little dishes containing food, whose
ingredients included the flesh of these animals, were placed over
palm leaves on the floor of the big room. We went back inside and
quietly shared a meal with the rest of the crowd.

Three weeks later I interviewed Leticia/Iemanjá and her "father"
(**Babalorixá**) Pai Saponan de Omolú. A small and delicate white
woman in her late thirties, her black hair beginning to grow back
after being shaved for initiation, Leticia told me she had only blurred
memories of her **Saida de Iaô**. She said she had sought initiation
because she was continually fainting at work (she was a clerk at a
local University) and "doctors could not find anything wrong with
me". She had a recurrent nightmare in which she drowned. It
became "so bad" that she was afraid to fall asleep. The doctors prescribed Valium but she was so drugged out that she started missing
work. She thought she was going mad. A co-worker suggested she
visit a Candomblé house. She came to Pai Saponan's house on the
outskirts of the city of Campinas and she fainted during a public
ceremony. Cida, the Little Mother of the House, carried her out to
the patio, and later told her she had fallen into trance. Pai Saponan
had read the oracle (Búzios) and identified the **Orixá Iemanjá** as
the "owner of her head", who wanted to take residence in Leticia.

After initiation Leticia said she does not faint at work anymore
although sometimes she feels dizzy and either she goes home or
she lays down in the employee's lounge. According to Leticia, her

co-workers, many of whom attend the same Candomblé house and therefore have a kinship relationship with her, "(they) understand what is going on with me and take over my duties when I get 'bolada' (in mild trance). And I do the same with them".

Leticia's dramatic transformation from the clerk, lower class petite white woman, to the imposing **Orixá Iemanjá** aroused my interest in the cult. At the time I was researching the process of character construction and embodiment by actors and stage performers cross-culturally. Different from Leticia's transformation into Iemanjá, actors' transformation into characters supposes "intention". In Western theatrical tradition, actors' transformations are always intentional in the sense that they are subject to the actor's will and a consciousness of the self is maintained. The "unintentional" dramatic transformation set off by trance, as exemplified by Leticia, prompts a different set of questions, the most important of which is: What are the mechanisms by which Leticia's "unintended" dramatic transformation make possible the construction of an alternative identity?

Most of my research was conducted in the Ketu house of Pai Saponan de Omolú in the city of Campinas, São Paulo from 1987 to 1989. The Saponan's *terreiro* is in Campinas, a college town 100 km from São Paulo, the largest city in the country. The members of the Candomblé house are mostly white, low/middle class, and a majority work at the University of Campinas. Although Pai Saponan follows a Ketu liturgy, he is not worried about issues of "purity" which concern other "traditional" Candomblé houses. As he says: "We all know that Jesus Christ **is not Oxalá**, but that actually Jesus Christ **belongs to Oxalá**".

What is Candomblé?

Candomblé is one among many African derived religions practiced today in Brazil. The cult is widely diffused and extends from small cities to the metropoles across the country. Researchers from the University of São Paulo reported 3,000 houses of Candomblé in 1989 in the city of São Paulo alone (Prandi and Gonçalves, 1989). Initially a black, female, and lower class phenomenon, today Candomblé includes women and men from a wide range of ethnic, class, and educational backgrounds.

Candomblé establishes an internal hierarchy through constructed kinship groups based on ritual adoption. Each "family" claims a particular space as a household, the **terreiro**. In a larger scale, relations between Candomblé households show corporate overtones as well as links to common ancestors (mythical and human), thus suggesting descent and ethnic groups.

Demonstrating a feature also characteristic of the African animist religions, Candomblé repudiates differentiations between the supernatural and everyday life, and between the body and the mind; the crossroad between the sacred and the profane is the human body in performance. "Performance" is here defined as a stylized repetition of actions resulting in a synthesis of behavior and meaning constituted in time. Constantly shifting bodily gestures, movements, enactments, and language convey peoples' identities, which are socially constituted. In this sense, subjects **perform** their identities, which are neither seamless nor essential but intrinsically discontinuous and arbitrary. Thus identity is not an inner essence, but a general consistency in action over time, a style of self-presentation that is performed: a style of talking, interacting, and moving (Stromberg, 1993).

During Candomblé ceremonies, dance and music trigger states of trance in which humans embody the gods. Such embodiment has historically permitted the survival, transformation and re-creation of Candomblé's body of meanings. In the following discussion, I examine the phenomenon of trance during the initiation process and suggest a connection between Candomblé's use of the body in performance and alternative constructions of social identities *vis-à-vis* the Brazilian State. Such construction of identities, and their resulting empowerment, originate in the training of the human body for trance/performance as the crossroad between mythical and social worlds.

The human body is the battleground where structures of power in society are challenged. This paper examines identity as a performance accomplishment compelled by a whole body of practices and expectations, over the whole of living prescribed by society and internalized by the subjects (**hegemony**), and suggests that the possibility of identity transformation challenges these hegemonic practices, meanings, and values through performance.

Recovering the Body

In Brazil, the development of capitalism required the dissolution of economic and social relationships of the plantation system based upon the bodies of slaves as commodities. The body of the slave, a perishable commodity, was ideologically constructed as an extension of the body of the master.

It was only during the dissolution of the colonial order and the "freeing" of the slaves that the bodies of the latter began to be considered complex machines, rather like Euro-bodies. The regulation of the "free" blacks became a concern of the state through their construction as a citizens; the black/slave trope was transformed into black/worker/citizen of the Brazilian State. At the same time, the identification of slaves as blacks, lazy, dirty, and stupid was maintained. The characterization of blacks as "physical" as opposed to "intellectual", and of their sexuality as "animal" and "promiscuous" was a result of the colonial fetishistic treatment of black bodies recast in new terms. These fundamental class, racial, and sexual markers implicated in a wider set of colonial relations of power were reproduced in the consolidation of capitalist social relations.

The constitution of blacks as slaves, based on their labor, articulated a process of integration of the "Africans" regardless of their particular national or cultural origins. The slaves, their cultural links severed from their own societies, adopted from each other practices and meanings that could be recreated in the colony. Many of these originated in religion. Yoruba religious rituals brought by slaves from West Africa were based both on lineages originating in a divine ancestor (**Orixá**) and in fellowship (**confrarías**). When lineages were broken by slavery, fellowship became the means for the creation of ritual. The Candomblé community established hierarchies based on the mother/child bond and re-constituted its lineages through ritual adoption. The slaves appropriated the notion of "slave family" imposed on them by the colonial state and created a site of resistance where they re-defined their own identities through the medium of ritual performance.

Under the category of workers, people of different racial, cultural, and national origins were thrust together and assembled into neighborhoods where they created different forms of communal organization. In this way, the slave/black house of Candomblé evolved to its present form as a neighborhood center of communal activity where alternative identities are constructed and performed in contradiction to the racial and gender parameters imposed by the Brazilian State.

Initiation, Public Ceremonies and Trance

The initiation of Leticia/Iemanjá consisted of a secret re-training of her body anchored in the Candomblé world view which was re-cast historically through slavery. Slave trade brought people to Brazil from three different regions: West Africa, Angola, and Mozambique. The "tribal" origins of Candomblé can be traced today to the different linguistic "nations" or cult groups, which also present slight differences in cosmology and liturgy. The slaves, who came from different regions of Africa and spoke different languages, had in common the use of the body as the instrument for social and divine communication. Below I discuss some features of the Yoruba/Ketu branch of Candomblé developed primarily from Yoruba beliefs. This particular branch uses an archaic form of Yoruba as ritual language: it is followed in the terreiro of Pai Saponan de Omolú.

Candomblé includes diverse West African, as well as Catholic, Kardecist (Spiritism) and Indian beliefs. Yoruba religions and Catholicism have many common traits that permitted an early juxtaposition. In Candomblé cosmology, **axé** is the life force possessed by everything existing in the Universe. Its source is **Olorún**, the only god, creator of existence, who does not partake of human affairs. Under **Olorún**, the abode of the sacred is populated by the **Orixás** who are deified male and female ancestors and/or personified natural forces. The **Orixás**, who form a mythical kinship group, express their particular life forces (**axés**) through the phenomenon of trance. The Orixá chooses an individual to be his or her "horse". Through the chosen person the Orixá visits the worshippers and receives their offerings. In Brazil, the "horse" is acknowledged by the Orixa as a descendant, regardless of race, gender or age. Every person has two Orixás, a dominant one and a secondary one. The physical features and personality of each individual originate from the specific quality of the **axés** of his/her Orixás. Each person is considered unique and manifests a unique quality of the Orixás they embody; therefore, there are as many different qualities or manifestations as there are individuals. Personality and the human body are not seen as static states but as moments of a process of dialogue in which the person and the Orixá develop their relationship through performance. The Orixá is in a "raw" state (**estádo bruto**) in all of us. It takes initiation and the continuous performance of ritual obligations to "settle" it down (**assentar o santo**) in ourselves.

During her initiation, a seventeen day retreat, Leticia was trained to embody historically determined cultural meanings, which go against both her commodification as a person and her capacity for productive work. Initiation is a time of deep coexistence with the Orixá, when the "public" "essential" identity, defined by the Brazilian State, is weakened and abandoned in favor of a divine and mythical one. The ceremonies during this period are secret, only witnessed by the **Ialorixá/Babalorixá**, who is the head of the terreiro, the Little Mother (a second in command in the hierarchy of the house), and the senior daughters and sons of the house.

At the beginning of the retreat, Leticia's head and body hair was shaved, and the top of her head received a tiny incision marking the re-opening of the fontanel. Birds and other animals were sacrificed and their blood was poured on Leticia's head. She also drank a small amount of it. At this moment, Leticia, as is usually the case with most novices, experienced a violent trance followed by fainting. On the third day, Leticia went out of the seclusion room (**camarinha**), her body and head painted with white dots and covered with a white sheet. The third day ceremony includes dancing to the drums and the sacred songs, after which Leticia went back into seclusion. On the seventh day, Leticia's head was painted blue; the ceremony was similar to that of the third day. The "**Naming Ceremony**" takes place the third time novices come out of seclusion. Leticia, in a state of semi-consciousness, was asked by her **Babalorixá**, Pai Saponan, to state her new name. Leticia, quietly dancing with the Little Mother, who was playing the **adjá** (a small metallic bell which facilitates trance), whispered "**Inaé**" which is the quality of her particular Iemanjá. Pai Saponan asked twice more. On the third time, Leticia shouted "Inaé". The members of the house, yelled back the proper Yoruba salutation for Iemanjá: Odo-iya-é. Everybody began singing and Leticia danced in a full-out trance until she was about to faint. At this point, the Little Mother calmed her and took her back into seclusion. Leticia insists that she does not remember anything of her "Naming Ceremony".

During the initiation period novices experience three different trance states. In the prevalent mild trance, the novice is semi-conscious but does not talk, move or eat. During the full trance the novice dances, experiences high vibratory movement, and finally faints. Between trance and normality, the novice undergoes an intermediate state known as **Erê**. In the state of **Erê**, the novice behaves like a playful child. **Erê** allows the novices to regain some of the physiological functions that are suspended during mild and full trance such as eating, sleeping, and speaking.

Novices, in the childish state of **Erê**, undergo a period of training in all the everyday activities before returning to normal life. Pai Saponan explained to me that the **Erê** recognizes all the tasks of the novice in normal state but approaches them with a total lack of interest. The **Erê** does not establish emotional or moral connections with a past life. When novices return to their former lives, the aspects of the Orixás are now embedded in their personalities. After returning to their normal activities, novices remember only a few details about the initiation period. In this extended transitional phase "profane social relations may be discontinued, former rights and obligations are suspended" (Turner, 1982, p. 27).

Through initiation, the novice is reborn within a new kinship group and partakes of a new ethnic identity: the people-of-saint (**povo de santo**). The Ialorixá/Babalorixá, through the reopening of the fontanel, the blood baptism, and the "Naming Ceremony" becomes the novice's mother/father. The Little Mother provides the motherly care and training for the "newborn". Novices who share the initiation process simultaneously are siblings. The senior daughters/sons are now older brothers and sisters. After the initiation the relationships with the biological family lose importance, and the new relatives, now addressed by kin terms, acquire primacy in terms of solidarity, obedience, respect, etc. The novices, who during initiation are placed beyond social norms, become members of a group. This group has constructed a set of rules in contradiction to those which define people as subjects of the Brazilian State. Candomblé's ethnic self-definition, independent of the actual race of its members, develops networks of adoptive kin for pursuing individual and communal utilities; it also provides a powerful motivation for collective activity (Comaroff, 1987).

The culminating ceremony of Leticia/Iemanjá's initiation, **Saida de Iaô**, is an example of a public Candomblé ceremony. Different public ceremonies have a similar format, starting with the private sacrifice of animals and the offerings to **Exú**, the Messenger of the Orixás, and including singing, percussion, and dance.

The dance consists of simple rhythmic movements that are repeated in a counter clockwise circle ad infinitum. The accompaniment by three drums and the **adjá**, as well as the movements, change as each Orixá is invoked. The gestures of each dance represent the personalities of each of the Orixás. For instance, the Orixá

Iemanjá, "owner of Leticia's head", moves her arms suggesting the motions of the sea, since she is the Lady of the Oceans. She displays her beauty and vanity in the way she carries her body and demands gifts from the worshippers that enhance her appearance, such as perfumes and mirrors, as well as her favorite foods.

The repetitive movement in a circular pattern creates a rhythm conducive to "divine possession" or flow. The merging of action and awareness of the flow of experience is made possible by centering attention on a limited field of stimuli (Turner, 1982). This intensification of consciousness extends the here and now, opening the access to the mythical time of the Orixás.

Trance gives way to the arrival of the Orixás. At this point, the person dances with energy; the expression of the face changes; the eyes are closed; the gestures reveal the presence of the Orixá. The transformation is complete. The person becomes "someone else". The body, taken to the extreme of its endurance, begins to shake; the person folds inward and faints on the floor. Finally, if the person is not attended, the body arches back and becomes rigid. Attendants take the person inside the **camarinha** where he/she is costumed with the clothes and objects of his/her particular Orixá: for instance, Iemanjá, whose ritual objects are a metallic fan and a short sword, wears blue and white clothes and collars of transparent beads. The living Orixá re-enters the large room where the ceremony is taking place and is greeted by the participants with the appropriate salutations. The Orixá dances in a stereotyped manner until he/she is overcome with physical exhaustion. After the ceremony the "horse" recuperates through a state of childish detachment (**Erê**). The individual does not remember the full trance experience.

The Orixás have complex mythological relations among them. When more than one Orixá is manifest in the dance, these mythical connections emerge in the form of a sacred drama. These mythical dramas are the vehicle for the constant re-creation of cultural identity for their participants (Turner, 1980).

Conclusion

Candomblé posits the body in trance as a crossroad between visible and invisible realities and as a receptacle of the **axé** (life force) of the Orixás. The connection between the visible and the invisible takes place in a multiplicity of sites. In the human body, the head (**orí**) provides the residence of the individual axé. Time acts as a second layer of Candomblé's sacred geography. Time, defined as a continuum, permits the coexistence of the deified ancestors and the members of the cult through trance.

The transmission and development of the axé from the Orixás to the humans takes place through trance/performance. Trance can be defined as psycho-kinesthetic phenomenon that arises in the pelvis, torso and throat, simultaneously shifting the elements of the personality, which culminates in a performance of the stories of the Orixás. The main ritual focus in Candomblé is on the preparation of the individual to experience trance through the process of initiation.

The process of initiation allows the Orixá to take possession of the head of the individual. During initiation the person undergoes a "training" which prepares his/her body to fully receive the Orixá. This "training" is grounded in a concept of the body which challenges the hegemonic notions of body, mind, identity, race, gender, and citizenship.

In Candomblé the body is a receptacle for the deity in which the identity of the person intermingles with the identity of the orixá in a new undifferentiated synthesis, a synthesis constituted in time through a stylized repetition of acts which we call performance. The body comes to bear cultural and historical meanings, and the manner of this bearing is fundamentally *dramatic*, what Judith Butler has called a "continual and incessant materializing of possibilities" (Butler, 1990).

The "training" during Candomblé initiation is directed to the embodiment of this "continual and incessant materializing of possibilities", the generation of an alternative identity. Trance cannot be explained as a role played by the person, because it is not expressive but performative. Identity itself is performative because it is real only to the extent that it is performed. The distinction between expression and performance is crucial. Expression denotes the enactment of a series of behaviors, gestures and ways of speaking that reveal a substantial pre-existing core of identity. This is the hegemonic notion of identity encouraged by the State: our citizenship and political rights (or lack thereof), our gender and race, are fixed and quantifiable in advance. Thus our gestures, ways of speaking and behaving are an expression of the different ways in which we deal with purportedly "natural" parameters. In contrast, the construction of alternative identities in Candomblé clearly indicates the fact that being black or white, woman or man, homosexual or hetero-sexual, mentally ill or healthy, is not "natural" to our identity but is a product of a concrete historical construct **that can be reinter-preted and challenged**. When we say that the various ways in which the body produces cultural signification in Candomblé is performative, we mean that there is no such thing as a prior **essential** identity waiting to be expressed. As opposed to a view which assumes a self that exchanges various roles within complex social pressures, the process of constructing Candomblé identities suggest that the self is socially constituted and constantly shifting.

Herein lies the main challenge posed by Candomblé to the hege-monic notions of personhood defined by the Brazilian State: the human body seen as a continuous embodiment of possibilities through a stylized repetition of acts openly contradicts the idea that identity is a fixed core or locus from which various acts originate. Candomblé makes explicit that the ways in which the body is set to conform are socially compelled. They are not part of an "under-lying natural" or intrinsic reality. Identity is what we assume everyday, under constraint, anxiety, or pleasure; it is repeatedly reproduced through prescribed social performances. Thus, it is through performance that Candomblé challenges these hegemonic practices, meanings and values.

Glossary

Adjá: small metallic bell used in Candomblé ceremonies. Its sound provokes trance in the participants.

Assentar o santo: "Settling down" or establishing the Orixá in a novice's head. It is accomplished through the process of initiation.

Axé: Life force.

Babalorixá/Ialorixá: Father-of-saint/Mother-of-saint. Head of a Candomblé household.

Barracão: Large room with a central pole where Candomblé public ceremonies take place.

Bolada: Candomblé jargon for "mild trance".

Búzios: Oracle. It consists of a number of shells that are thrown at random. It is used to predict the future and to determine a per-son's Orixás.

Candomblé: An African-derived religion practiced today in Brazil, with certain similarities to Umbanda in other parts of Brazil, Haitian "voudoo", and Afro-Cuban Santeria.

Camarinha: Small room where novices are secluded during their initiation. It is also used as a dressing room for public ceremonies.

Confrarías: Fellowships of association.

Estádo bruto: "Raw state". Orixás are said to be in their estado bruto when they have still not been "settled down" in a person.

Erê: State of childish detachment that follows trance.

Exú: Messenger of the Orixás. Every ceremony starts with an invocation to Exú. Syncretic equivalent of the Devil.

Hegemony: Concept developed in the work of Antonio Gramsci (1927–35) that has become one of the major turning-points in Marxist cultural theory. It recasts the articulation between dominance and subordination as "a whole body of practices and expectations over the whole of living" (Williams, 1977: 110). For lucid discussions of hegemony see Raymond Williams (1977), William Roseberry (1994), and Derek Sayer (1994).

Iemanjá: Mother of the Orixás. Lady of the Ocean. Syncretic equivalent of the Immaculate Conception.

Inaê: A quality of Iemanjá.

Ketu: Yoruba branch of Candomblé.

Laro-iê Exú: Salutation to Exú.

Odo-iya-é: Salutation to Iemanjá.

Omolú: Orixá of disease, specifically small-pox. Syncretic equivalent of St. Lazarus.

Olorún: God.

Orí: The human head in Yoruba. The environment of the Orixás.

Orixá: Deified ancestor or force of nature who visits mortals through trance. Syncretic equivalent of catholic saints.

Oxalá: Father of the Orixás. Syncretic equivalent of Jesus Christ.

Pai Saponan de Omolú: Father Saponan of Omolú. Head of the *terreiro* in Campinas where this research was conducted. His main Orixá is Omolú in the quality of Saponan.

Povo de santo: Literally "people of saint", i.e., Candomblé adepts.

Saida de Iaô: "Exit of novice". Culminating ceremony of a Candomblé initiation.

Terreiro: House of Candomblé, where the ceremonies occur.

References

Butler, Judith (1990) "Performative Acts and Gender Constitution: An Essay in Phenomenology and Feminist Theory" in S. Case (Ed.), *Performing Feminisms: Feminist Critical Theory and Theatre*. Baltimore: The John Hopkins University Press.

Comaroff, John (1987) "Of Totemism and Ethnicity: Consciousness, Practice and the Signs of Inequality", *Ethnos*, **52**: 3–4, 301, 323.

Prandi, Reginaldo and V. Goncalves (1989) "Deuses Tribais de Sao Paulo", in *Ciencia Hoje*. Brasilia: CNPq.

Roseberry, William (1994) "Hegemony and the language of contention", in G. Joseph and D. Nugent (Eds.) *Everyday Forms of State Formation*. Durham: Duke University Press.

Sayer, Derek (1994) "Everyday forms of state formation: Some dissident remarks on 'hegemony'", in G. Joseph and D. Nugent (Eds.) *Everyday Forms of State Formation*. Durham: Duke University Press.

Stromberg, Peter G. (1993) *Language and Self Transformation: A Study of the Christian Conversion Narrative*. Cambridge: Cambridge University Press.

Turner, Victor (1980) "Social Dramas and Stories About Them", in *From Ritual to Theatre: The Human Seriousness of Play*. New York: Paj Publications.

——. (1982) "Liminal to Liminoid in Play, Flow, and Ritual: An Essay in Comparative Symbology", in *From Ritual to Theatre: The Human Seriousness of Play*. New York: Paj Publications.

Williams, Raymond (1977) *Marxism and Literature*. New York: Oxford University Press.

Zorrilla-Tessler Eva C. (1988–89) Unpublished field notes from the terreiro do Pai Saponan de Omolú, Campinas S.P. Brazil.

Choreography and Dance
1998, Vol. 5, Part 1, pp. 117–127
Photocopying permitted by license only

Places Where I've Been: Reflections on Issues of Gender in Dance Education, Research, and Administration

Susan W. Stinson

The private domain of personal experience has often been left out of scholarly research because of gender bias. This paper critically reflects upon the author's experiences as a professional dance educator, researcher, and administrator, using a lens of feminist analysis. Through this analysis, the author becomes aware of the appeal of traditional gendered expectations and how she has participated in them at the same time that she has struggled against them. She concludes that bringing personal narratives into the public domain, and placing them in a context of feminist interpretation, can allow women not only to understand their lives, but to transform them.

KEY WORDS   Gender, dance education, dance research, dance administration, feminist analysis.

I learned as a young girl that it is impolite to talk about oneself. I learned as a student that it is inappropriate to make personal disclosures in an academic paper. I learned as a young adult that it is unprofessional to share private stories with colleagues. I am about to break these prohibitions, all of which are rooted in gender issues. Feminists have noted that the public domain, that of facts and figures and abstract theories, has long been considered the province of men, while the private domain, that of home and family, personal experience and feelings, has been considered the province of women. Because men hold power in academia, the private domain has been perceived as inappropriate for scholarly work. As Madeleine Grumet (1988) noted, when we attempt to emulate the "elitism of the other 'professions,' we subscribe to patriarchy's contempt for the familiar, the personal" (p. 58). Grumet's own work provides an excellent

117

model for weaving the private domain of personal experience into scholarly discourse. I follow such a model in this paper as I reflect on my personal experience in three of the professional roles I occupy, as a dance educator, a researcher, and an administrator.

Issues in Dance Education

I came of age in the 1960s, saw that many non-traditional careers were now open to women, and vowed that I would not become a teacher. Nevertheless, I have been a dance educator for over 25 years, first as a teacher of children and adolescents, now as a teacher of prospective teachers and other students, both undergraduate and graduate. My interest in gender in dance education was sparked by my discovery of the concept of the hidden curriculum, which refers to what students are learning aside from what teachers are explicitly teaching. By examining my own experience, I was able to identify issues of gender hidden within dance pedagogy.

One of these issues was passivity and obedience: An agenda in most dance teaching is that students learn to be good little girls who stand in straight lines and do as they are told. The obedience required in professional ballet training which keeps young women both physically and emotionally in a pre-pubescent state is well documented (Brady, 1982; Gordon, 1983; Innes, 1988; Kirkland, 1986; Vincent, 1979). Since I am not directly involved in this part of the dance world, it would have been easy to simply blame those who are. Through reflection on my personal experience, however, I was able to recognize why this passive role is so appealing and powerful. Ten years ago I wrote,

I see them come into the room for freshman orientation, the girl-children who will major in dance. I see faces and bodies that know how to be good, who like to do what they are told and are successful at it. Even when we as teachers try to challenge them to find new ways to move, to think, there is reluctance to move from being pretty and graceful children who do what they are told. I know why, not from looking at them, but from looking at myself. There is a kind of freedom in obedience, the freedom from responsibility. I appreciate it now when my days seem so full of responsibility, full of solving problems, making class assignments and grading scales as well as dentist appointments and carpool arrangements. What a relief to have someone tell me what to do. I take a dance technique class, and revel in the luxury of feeling active yet passive. She tells and shows everything I need to do. It is like having someone else feed me.

It is surely no sin to recognize one's own weariness, and the need for sustenance for an arduous journey. But how easy it is to lose sight of the journey in those delicious moments, and begin to think that we have made a real accomplish-ment ... in digesting someone else's milk (revised from Stinson, 1984, pp. 89–90).

Obedience usually means silence in listening to others, in order to do as one is told. Mary Belenky and colleagues (1986) point out that adult women are silenced much more often than men. In their analysis, "finding one's voice" is a metaphor frequently used when women describe their own journeys from silence to critical thinking; for women, learning to think means learning to speak with their own voice. Traditional dance pedagogy, with its emphasis on silent conformity, does not facilitate such a journey. Dancers typically learn to reproduce what they receive, not to critique or create. And yet, as I recognized, there is something appealing in this position.

My realization of my own desire for the security of obedience was painful. Equally so was the recognition that forms of pedagogy which I cherished, even creative dance for children, are not free from this issue. Certainly creative dance teaches self-expression and problem solving rather than passivity. It is important to remember, however, that creative dance derives from the values of the progressive education movement earlier in this century. While progressive pedagogy avoids the coercion of authoritarian methods, its goals are similar: producing docile, well-disciplined individuals who will fit into the way things are, rather than attempt to change them. Valerie Walkerdine (1992) notes that progressive education established the schoolroom (and, one might add, the children's dance studio) as

a laboratory, where development could be watched, monitored and set along the right path. There was therefore no need for ... discipline of the overt kind .... The classroom became the facilitating space for each individual, under the watchful and total gaze of the teacher, who was held responsible for the development of each individual. (pp. 17–20)

It was hard for me to realize how creative dance did not resolve the issue of docility, but simply made it harder to recognize.

Escapism

Walkerdine describes the classroom environment of progressive educators as a place where children are taught to be not only docile, but also happy:

[In such a classroom] the children are only allowed happy sentiments and happy words ... There is a denial of pain, oppression ... There is also a denial of power, as though the helpful teacher didn't wield any. (1992, p. 20)

This statement raises the possibility of a connection between escapism (from a painful and oppressive world) and powerlessness. My own experience illustrates these themes. Underlying the following story, which I wrote in 1986, is the sense of being helpless in the face of the Big Problems of the world, choosing instead a path that gives us a limited sense of power but also supports the larger problems by making them easier to tolerate:

> I remember when I first made the decision to become a dance educator, [as] a senior … sociology major [intending] to continue for a graduate degree in social work. The year was 1968, one filled with racial unrest and urban violence. The only people in social work who seemed to be making any difference were those in the field known as community action, living in the poorest of urban neighborhoods to help residents begin to find control over their own lives. As a young, middle-class white woman, I was afraid to take on such a role.
>
> At the same time I was tutoring a small group of poor children, with whom I also did some dance activities. I felt powerless to do anything about the larger socio-economic picture that drew lines between us, making me one of the haves and them the have-nots. But in our dance class I could share my love for dance, and possibly serve as a role model for these children. Egocentrically, I thought that if only the children could be like me, all their problems would be solved.
>
> Since that time I have become not only a dance educator but a mother. I often find myself in conversations with other mothers; at times we discuss the state of the world … All we can do is to take one small part of the world and try to make it beautiful or happy. The problems of poverty are too large—but I can give my own children, or those in my classes—a joyful childhood. (Stinson, 1986, pp. 7–8)

Historically, this has been the socially constructed role of women: to be the nurturers, the caregivers, the creators of small spots of beauty within an otherwise often bleak world. Women create homes, flower gardens, and sometimes even dances and, by and large, leave it to men to create major corporations and rule the world. And while we easily recognize that women in many cases have been denied real political power, as Dorothy Dinnerstein (1976) and Nancy Chodorow (1978) point out, this denial benefits women as well, freeing us from the risks and responsibilities of power.

The real world is often one of pain, ugliness, and danger. While all three may be present in the dance world, we can escape to corners of consciousness where we feel free. Some in dance escape into a world of beauty. Others escape into the world of self, allowing the image in the mirror, or achieving one more inch of elevation, to become the focus of existence.

It *is* more pleasant to look at little children dancing snowflakes than to look at victims of child abuse. It is easier to assure progress in strength, flexibility, and coordination than to assure progress toward world peace. And the transcendent experience of dance can make us feel so whole that it becomes the only part of our lives that seems real and important.

The Nature/Culture Dichotomy

Another gender issue in dance education has to do with the prioritizing of culture over nature. A number of feminist theorists have pointed out that the human body and nature (as in Mother Nature and Mother Earth) are more closely connected with women, while the mind and culture are regarded as the province of men (Jaggar, 1983). While we would have a difficult time determining what a "natural" body is, a cultural aesthetic guides our ideas of what a dancer's body should look like. The current Western dance aesthetic demands a long, thin body, carried to the extreme in ballet, a body that is not natural for many women. Many choreographers and directors encourage and even demand the "anorexic look." The same is increasingly true in modern dance, with many professional modern dancers now regarding the ballet class as their basic form of training and many modern dance choreographers setting their work on ballet companies. Even among young women in non-professional classes, criticism of one's body is part of the expected behavior. Judy Alter, in a 1986 study, noted that weight occurred as a topic in 18 of the 31 classes she studied. In a 1990 study I co-authored, the young dancers made such comments about their bodies as, "I don't like my body, the way it looks"; "Lots of time I think I'm too much of a brute to be a dancer"; and "If my legs matched my body then I'd be perfectly happy" (Stinson, Blumenfeld-Jones, Van Dyke, 1990, p. 17). Surely such feelings about the body are enhanced by a pedagogy in which the goal is an unattainable ideal and all attempts are met with corrections indicating how one does not measure up. All this happens while one is looking in a mirror, dressed in clothing that reveals every flaw.

I remember when I began to make a conscious decision to stand off to the side in technique class, so I could not see myself in the mirror. Was this an act of courage, allowing me to focus on what I most valued in dancing, kinesthetic sensing of the movement, or an admission of defeat in a battle for the kind of body I had wanted since third grade? In Western dance culture, the body often seems to be regarded as an enemy to be overcome or an object to be judged. However, dance training merely intensifies the values of the larger social world. In our society, while overweight is dreaded by all and the body is regarded as an enemy by both men and women who exercise compulsively and obsessively, women's bodies are more often identified as objects to be looked at and judged.

In summary, then, I have identified three gender issues in dance education: passivity/obedience, escapism from a sense of power-lessness, and a dominance of culture over nature. I have been one of many suggesting that such conditions limit the personhood of the women we educate in dance, often beginning at such an early age that we can hardly claim they had a choice. Despite this, we all continue to consent to such arrangements.

Issues in Dance Research

As a researcher for the past ten years, I participate in what is con-sidered an occupation of the mind. The mind/body duality, which mirrors the culture/nature duality I have already discussed, gives greater prestige to mind. In our society, women have been largely charged with the care of the bodily needs of others: the caretaking of the young and the elderly, preparing meals, doing the laundry. Although many men participate in physical labor (where their larger, stronger bodies are more highly valued than those of women), the most prestigious work is carried out by those who work with their minds, not their hands.

Certainly men's work (whether physical labor or work of the mind) is consistently valued more highly in our society than women's work; salary differentials between jobs traditionally held by women and those held by men provide some evidence of this. The perception of men's work vs. women's work becomes partic-ularly interesting when one considers the three primary duties of university faculty: teaching, research, and service. Teaching and service have, at least in recent history, been viewed primarily as women's work. Both involve caretaking and significant inter-personal contact, putting one's personal needs aside to meet the needs of others. Research, on the other hand, can often be done individually, "every man for himself." While certainly there is a current trend toward collaborative research in many fields, the dilemma for individual faculty has often been symbolized by the office door: Should it be open, allowing students to enter, or closed to allow for doing one's own work? Like that of many women, my image of the teacher is like my idea of the mother. Good teachers, like good mothers, are available when they are needed. Similarly, good members of departments and committees make themselves available for the unpleasant tasks that need to get done, out of regard for the community and the relationships that hold it together.

At most research universities, however, it is research that counts the most in promotion and tenure decisions. Some in higher education have questioned whether policies that prioritize research over teaching and service discriminate against women, who devote more time to teaching and service and are rated higher in these activities. As Grumet notes, "schooling supports the dominance of men in society…by gradually establishing success norms that favor males, linking their achievements and world views to ideologies that dominate both the economy and the state" (1988, p. 45).

Like many women in a university, I have learned to play by the rules made by men. By doing this, I have gained tenure and the rank of full professor, all the while working extra hours to satisfy my service ethic. However, women are also disproportionately responsible for caregiving in the home, and I am no exception. I learned to neglect my own personal needs in order to parent as well as teach and do research and provide service. Marilyn Loden cites a business executive who states, "Women at the executive level must often sacrifice their sleep and leisure time in order to succeed as parents and professionals" (1985, p. 208). I think that this is an apt description, as well, of women who try to climb the tenure track while simultaneously taking care of everyone but themselves. As Grumet writes, "For those who sustain the emotional and physical lives of others, there is no time out, no short week, no sabbatical, no layoffs." (1988, p. 85)

Another gender issue in research relates to the validity of academic knowledge. Because my focus is dance education, a combination of two areas considered low status because they are largely populated by women, my research is immediately suspect. Further, I use what Robert Donmoyer (1985) refers to as a humanities-based rather than a science based method, marking it as methodologically "soft" rather than "hard." My research focuses on the lived experiences of students, how they are making sense of their dance education experiences in the context of their lives. This represents an attempt to bring the voices of those in education with the least status, k-12, mostly female students, into the literature. I recall the response of the acting Dean of Research to my application for research leave several years ago: "How can you learn anything from listening to a bunch of high school students?" From his vantage point, my work had little chance to contribute to the body of knowledge in academe. And his was the final voice in determining who was allowed research leave.

Nadya Aisenberg and Mona Harrington elucidate this incident:

A large body of women's work in the academy is marked by common, distinct characteristics: the loyalty to "soft" subjects in the humanities as indispensable to examining human values; the placement of subject matter in a cultural context;...the expansion of the canon in all fields by the validation of material previously overlooked or considered irrelevant; a strong emphasis on women's studies. (1988, p. 105)

They further note that

such...scholarship entails serious risks. The lingering association of women with lowly tasks, the ever-ready assumption of the inferiority of women's minds, make it easy to dismiss their unconventional work as unsubstantial. (p. 106)

I still struggle over whether to leave my door open or closed, and how to advise the women faculty I mentor regarding the risks they will be taking if they choose to do the kind of research both they and I value.

Issues in Dance Administration

In my newest role as a Department Head, I am expected to "manage" a department with nine other full-time positions and several part-time ones. The faculty, entirely female when I arrived 16 years ago, is now half male. I reluctantly accepted the role as Head out of that sense of responsibility women so often feel. I find two major parts to this management job, leadership (the traditional men's role) and housekeeping.

In terms of the latter, the job involves so much "women's work" that I am surprised that the vast majority of Heads in my university (about 85%) are male. Undoubtedly some of my counterparts in other departments are not as conscientious about the housework. Upon reflection, I realize that I have defined my role as Head primarily as one of service, and it is as hard for me to set boundaries on my departmental caretaking as it is to set them as a mother.

Much of this work, of course, is dull, tedious and repetitious, like most housework. It is embarrassing, then, to acknowledge that it causes me less discomfort than those demands of the Headship which have to do with power.

In my university, as in most hierarchical organizations, the Department Head has ultimate responsibility for *everything* that happens in the department. The Head also has great power *over* other members of the department, power possessed only because one is Head; this is what management texts refer to as positional power. It is possible to be very autocratic in such areas as budgeting, recommending tenure and merit raises, scheduling of classes, and hiring and firing of graduate assistants and part-time faculty. I am uncomfortable with positional power and acknowledge that, within a talented faculty, my personal power (defined by management texts as competence and charisma) is no greater than that of many of my colleagues. I wonder to what extent my discomfort in using the power my position provides is related to gender. Telling other people what to do seems much easier for many of my male colleagues.

Certainly not all faculty feel "called," as I do, to service; some resist or resent doing the boring tasks. It seems to me that, somewhere inside, most adults still want a Mother; we do not want the kind who nags us to do our chores, but rather a mythological Mother who does them all herself without making us feel guilty. A female Department Head can easily become the focus of such longings. Further, some faculty value personal and academic freedom but not the responsibility that goes with it, raising the themes of individual freedom vs. collective responsibility which abound in gender literature.

As a girl-child, I learned how to please people; as a Department Head, I have learned that it is often not possible to make decisions that please everyone. As a girl-child, I learned to empathize with others. As a Department Head, I now experience the pain I sometimes cause others by the actions I need to take. Certainly, I had some of these kinds of experiences as a teacher and even as a parent; neither job is a popularity contest. In those cases, however, it was clear to me, my students, and my children that my age and/or expertise gave me some qualifications (personal power) they lacked. Now, as Head, I recognize that several of my colleagues could be in this position; indeed, some have been. What gives me the right to power over them, other than the bureaucratic institution of which we are all a part? I often wonder whether it is possible to *LIVE* as a feminist in such an institution.

Conclusions

Through critical reflection, I have come to some degree of consciousness about how I have constructed my professional roles in ways that emphasize traditional female values, often following what Grumet refers to as the "maternal ethos of altruism, self abnegation, and repetitive labor" (1988, p. 87). Since all women do not make the same constructions, what is to be gained by sharing one's personal experiences in a public setting, experiences which reveal vulnerability and questions rather than answers and expertise? What is to be gained by a recognition of how we are so often prisoners of our own (gendered) experience? Certainly it is problematic if such reflections are used as ammunition by those who would continue to victimize women. I suppose that one might look upon the consciousness-raising I have done as therapy, a first step in changing my behavior and my psyche so that I can "fit" better into the academic insitution in which I live, with less personal anguish. Indeed, helping people adjust has often been the purpose of therapy in our society.

My goal is to go beyond therapy to what Kenway and Modra refer to as critical consciousness raising: "analysis of the context of problem situations for the purpose of enabling people together to transform their reality, rather than merely understand it or adapt to it with less discomfort" (1992, p. 156). It will not be easy to create a new world when all that we are has been shaped by the old one. As Dorothy Dinnerstein (1976) reminds us, we benefit as well as suffer from the current arrangements. For example, the current arrangements free many of us from the risks and responsibilities of power, while allowing us to blame those who have assumed such burdens. Until we reflect on both what is appealing and what is oppressive in them, we are likely either to continue to assent to the status quo, or to create a new world as oppressive as the old one. Critical reflection is the beginning not only to changing ourselves, but also to changing institutions so that they become places where all of us, men and women, can live more fully human lives.

References

Aisenberg, N. and Harrington, M. (1988) *Women of Academe: Outsiders in the Sacred Grove*. Amherst: University of Massachusetts Press.

Alter, J. (1986) A field study of an advanced dance class in a private studio setting. *Dance Studies*. **10**, 49–97 (published by Center for Dance Studies, Les Bois, St. Peter, Jersey, Channel Islands, Britain).

Belenky, M.F., Clinchy, B.M., Goldberg, N.R., and Tarule, J.M. (1986) *Women's Ways of Knowing: The Development of Self, Voice, and Mind*. New York: Basic Books.

Brady, J. (1982) *The Unmaking of a Dancer: An Unconventional Life*. New York: Harper and Row.

Chodorow, N. (1978) *The Reproduction of Mothering*. Berkeley: University of California Press.

Dinnerstein, D. (1976) *The Mermaid and the Minotaur: Sexual Arrangements and the Human Malaise*. New York: Harper Colophon Books (Harper and Row).

Donmoyer, R. (1985) Distinguishing between scientific and humanities-based approaches to qualitative research. Paper presented at American Education Research Association annual meeting, Chicago.

Gordon, S. (1983) *Off-balance: The Real World of Ballet*. New York: Pantheon.

Grumet, M.R. (1988) *Bitter Milk: Women and Teaching*. Amherst: University of Massachusetts Press.

Innes, S. (1988, Winter) The teaching of ballet. *Writings on Dance*, **3**, 37–47.

Jaggar, A.M. (1983) *Feminist Politics and Human Nature*. Totowa, NJ: Rowman and Allanheld.

Kenway, J. and Modra, H. (1992) Feminist pedagogy and emancipatory possibilities. In *Feminisms and Critical Pedagogy*, edited by C. Luke and J. Gore, pp. 138–166. New York: Routledge.

Kirkland, G. with Lawrence, G. (1986) *Dancing on my Grave*. New York: Doubleday.

Loden, M. (1985) *Women in Leadership or How to Succeed in Business without Being One of the Boys*. New York: Times Books.

Stinson, S.W. (1984) *Reflections and Visions: A Hermeneutic Study of Dangers and Possibilities in Dance Education*. Doctoral dissertation, University of North Carolina at Greensboro.

——. (1987, March) Gender issues in dance education. In *Proceedings of the Fifth Curriculum Theory Conference in Physical Education*, edited by M.M. Carnes and P. Stueck, pp. 33–59. Athens: University of Georgia.

Stinson, S.W., Blumenfeld-Jones, D., and Van Dyke, J. (1990) Voices of young women dance students: An interpretive study of meaning in dance. *Dance Research Journal*. **22**(2), 13–22.

Vincent, L.M. (1979) *Competing with the Sylph: Dancers and the Pursuit of the Ideal Body Form*. Kansas City: Andrews and McMeel.

Walkerdine, V. (1992) Progressive pedagogy and political struggle. In *Feminisms and Critical Pedagogy*, edited by C. Luke and J. Gore, pp. 15–24. New York: Routledge.

Choreography and Dance
1998, Vol. 5, Part 1, pp. 129–132
Photocopying permitted by license only

Notes on Contributors

Bud Coleman is an Assistant Professor at the University of Colorado at Boulder in the Department of Theatre and Dance where he teaches Acting, American Theatre History, and Musical Theatre. At CU, Bud has directed/choreographed Lysistrata, Merrily We Roll Along, and Dames at Sea. Bud has a Ph.D. in Theatre History and Criticism from the University of Texas at Austin and has danced with Les Ballets Trockadero de Monte Carlo, Fort Worth Ballet, Ballet Austin, and Kinesis.

Ann Cooper Albright is a performer and feminist scholar, and an associate professor in the dance and theater program at Oberlin College, Ohio. She holds a B.A. in Philosophy from Bryn Mawr College, an M.F.A. in Dance from Temple University, and a Ph.D. in Performance Studies from New York University. Combining her interests in dancing and cultural theory, she is currently involved in teaching a variety of dance, performance studies and women's studies courses which seek to engage students in both the practice and the theory of the body. This fall, she is guest teaching a graduate seminar at Ohio State University entitled "Engaging Bodies: the Politics and Poetics of Corporeality." She was a recipient of a 1995 Ohio Arts Council Individual Artist Award in Dance Criticism. Her book, *Choreographing Difference: the Body and Identity in Contemporary Dance* was published by Wesleyan University Press in 1997.

Ann Daly is Associate Professor of Dance History/Criticism at The University of Texas at Austin. She has written on dance, gender, and culture for publications including: *TDR: A Journal of Performance Studies, Ballett International, Dance Research Journal, High Performance, Women and Performance, American Studies, Dance Theatre*

Journal, New York Times, and *Village Voice.* A past president of the Dance Critics Association, she is dance critic for *The Texas Observer* and co-book review editor of *TDR: A Journal of Performance Studies.* Her book, *Done into Dance: Isadora Duncan in America* (Indiana, 1995), was awarded the 1996 Congress On Research in Dance Award for Outstanding Publication.

Veta Goler, Associate Professor of Dance at Spelman College, has worked as a performer, choreographer, and teacher at various colleges and private studios around the country and Brazil. She holds a Ph.D. in African American Studies from Emory University and an M.F.A. in Dance from the University of Michigan. Her most significant recent choreographic and performance effort was *Skeletons Falling,* a concert of solos and duets presented in September 1995. She has given presentations about dance at dance research conferences, the Zora Neale Hurston Festival of the Arts, and at Jacobs Pillow Dance Festival. She has written about dance for *Dance Research Journal, High Performance,* and *EightRock.*

Kim Grover-Haskin, Doctoral Candidate in Dance and Related Arts at Texas Woman's University, has presented her research on dance and performance theory at meetings of the Congress on Research in Dance, American Dance Guild, National College Dance Festival, and the Northwest Arkansas Women's Festival. She presented a paper, *I'm a Stranger Here Myself: Dance for a Feminist Future,* at the June, 1994 meeting of the National Women's Studies Association. She received her B.S. in dance from the State University of New York at Potsdam and her M.S. in dance from the University of Oregon. She has served as a member of the TWU Women's Studies Core Curriculum Committee, and lectures for TWU Women's Studies courses. She coordinated and chaired a session on dance archives for the Society of Southwest Archivists and is currently conducting research in the area of feminist performance theory in dance.

Michie Hayashi was born in Japan, and graduated in 1962 from an Educational Course in the Literature Department of Nara Women's University. Between 1962–1973 she taught creative dance in senior high school in Osaka. Currently she is a professor of Osaka University of Health and Sport Sciences, teaching Dance History, Teaching Methods of Dance, Creative Dance for High School

Students (undergraduate program) and Communication Theory of Movements (graduate program). For 1976 to 1977 She was a visiting scholar at California State University, Sacrament and Mills College. She has been the Director of Teacher's Society of Dance Research in Osaka since 1980. From 1992 through 1994 she was the judge for the All Japan Dance Festival—Kobe. In 1994 she also became part time faculty of Nara Women's University. Her research has been in body image and expressive meaning, experimental research of anisotropy of dance space, the eye movement while watching dance movement and personality of dancers and athletes. Her publications have included The Method of Recreational Activity, The Lecture of Dance, Cross-Cultural Exchange in Dance: East/West (edited by Ruth Solomon & John Solomon), Illustrated Limon Technique (translated to Japanese), Children Dance in the Classroom (translated to Japanese) and Dance-Expressive Body and Mind.

Phylisé Smith has studied West African dance in Senegal, The Gambia and Ghana and is currently on the faculty of Scripps College and Orange Coast College in Southern California. Also, a performer, Smith dances with the West African dance group, The Serakumbili Project. Smith has presented and written several papers on West African dance in the United States and Africa.

Dr. Susan Stinson is Professor of dance at the University of North Carolina at Greensboro, where she serves as Department Head and teaches undergraduate courses in teacher preparation and graduate courses in research and curriculum. Her scholarly work has been published in a number of journals, including *Dance Research Journal*; *Design for Arts in Education*; *Impulse: The International Journal of Dance Science, Medicine, and Education*; *Journal of Physical Education, Recreation and Dance*; *Journal of Curriculum Theorizing*; *Women in Performance*; *Journal of Curriculum and Supervision*; *Educational Theory*; and *Drama/Dance*. For the past five years, her research has focused on how young people interpret their experiences in dance education in a school setting. Her book, *Dance for Young Children: Finding the Magic in Movement*, was published by AAHPERD and has also been published in Japanese. She has been active in a number of professional organizations, including the National Dance Association, Dance and the Child: International, and CORD (Congress on Research in Dance).

Eva Tessler, MFA in Theater Arts/Dance from the University of Arizona is a native of Mexico City. Ms. Tessler was a professor of dance at UNICAMP in Brazil from 1986–89 where she choreographed and danced extensively. Currently she teaches ballet at Tucson High School in Tucson, Arizona. Ms. Tessler is a member of the Zenith Dance Collective, a Tucson dance organization that produces much of her concert work. Highlights of her work include choreography for the World Premiere of the play *Old Matador* by Milcha Sanchez-Scott produced by the Arizona Theatre Company, movement for the film *Roosters* and co-authorship of the play *13 Days/13 Dias* which is currently on national tour in a production by the Award Winning San Francisco Mime Troupo. Ms. Tessler's choreography can also be seen in the Borderlands Theater production of Garcia Lorca's tragedies *Blood Wedding* and *Yerma*. She has published an article on Modern Dance, *O que e Danca Moderna?* for Revista Trilhas (1987, no. 2), Unicamp, Campinas, Brazil.

Judy Van Zile is a Professor of Dance at the University of Hawaii, where she coordinates the dance ethnology program. Her primary research interests are Asian dance, particularly dances of Korea; movement observation and analysis using Labanotation; Japanese *bon* dancing in Hawaii; change in traditional dance forms; and issues of identity. Judy conducted research in Korea in 1979, 1981, 1983, and 1990 under the auspices of the Korean Culture and Arts Foundation, Academy for Korean Studies, Fulbright Commission, and International Cultural Society of Korea. She is author of an annotated bibliography on dance in India and a monograph on Japanese *bon* dancing in Hawaii; editor of a collection of readings on dance in Africa, Asia, and the Pacific; and author of articles in books and serials on analysis of movement in *bharata natyam*, tourism and changes in *bon* dancing in Hawaii, Korean dance, and issues involved in using Labanotation.

Choreography and Dance
1998, Vol. 5, Part 1, pp. 133–142
Photocopying permitted by license only

Index

CHOREOGRAPHY AND DANCE
AN INTERNATIONAL JOURNAL

Notes for contributors

Submission of a paper will be taken to imply that it represents original work not previously published, that it is not being considered for publication elsewhere and that, if accepted for publication, it will not be published elsewhere in the same form, in any language, without the consent of editor and publisher. It is a condition of acceptance by the editor of a typescript for publication that the publisher automatically acquires the copyright of the typescript throughout the world. It will also be assumed that the author has obtained all necessary permissions to include in the paper items such as quotations, musical examples, figures, tables etc. Permissions should be paid for prior to submission.

Typescripts. Papers should be submitted in triplicate to the Editors, *Choreography and Dance*, c/o Harwood Academic Publishers, at:

5th Floor, Reading Bridge House	PO Box 32160	3-14-9, Okubo
Reading Bridge Approach	Newark	Shinjuku-ku
Reading RG1 8PP	NJ 07102	Tokyo 169-0072
UK or	USA or	Japan

Papers should be typed or word processed with double spacing on one side of good quality ISO A4 (212 × 297 mm) paper with a 3 cm left-hand margin. Papers are accepted only in English.

Abstracts and Keywords. Each paper requires an abstract of 100–150 words summarizing the significant coverage and findings, presented on a separate sheet of paper. Abstracts should be followed by up to six key words or phrases which, between them, should indicate the subject matter of the paper. These will be used for indexing and data retrieval purposes.

Figures. All figures (photographs, schema, charts, diagrams and graphs) should be numbered with consecutive arabic numerals, have descriptive captions and be mentioned in the text. Figures should be kept separate from the text but an approximate position for each should be indicated in the margin of the typescript. It is the author's responsibility to obtain permission for any reproduction from other sources.

Preparation: Line drawings must be of a high enough standard for direct reproduction; photocopies are not acceptable. They should be prepared in black (india) ink on white art paper, card or tracing paper, with all the lettering and symbols included. Computer-generated graphics of a similar high quality are also acceptable, as are good sharp photoprints ("glossies"). Computer print-outs must be completely legible. Photographs intended for halftone reproduction must be good glossy original prints of maximum contrast. Redrawing or retouching of unusable figures will be charged to authors.

Size: Figures should be planned so that they reduce to 12 cm column width. The preferred width of line drawings is 24 cm, with capital lettering 4 mm high, for reduction by one-half. Photographs for halftone reproduction should be approximately twice the desired finished size.

Captions: A list of figure captions, with the relevant figure numbers, should be typed on a separate sheet of paper and included with the typescript.

Musical examples: Musical examples should be designated as "Figure 1" etc., and the recommendations above for preparation and sizing should be followed. Examples must be well prepared and of a high standard for reproduction, as they will not be redrawn or retouched by the printer.

In the case of large scores, musical examples will have to be reduced in size and so some clarity will be lost. This should be borne in mind especially with orchestral scores.

Notes are indicated by superior arabic numerals without parentheses. The text of the notes should be collected at the end of the paper.

References are indicated in the text by the name and date system either "Recent work (Smith & Jones, 1987, Robinson, 1985, 1987)..." or "Recently Smith & Jones (1987)..." If a publication has more than three authors, list all names on the first occurrence; on subsequent occurrences use the first author's name plus "*et al.*" Use an ampersand rather than "and" between the last two authors. If there is more than one publication by the same author(s) in the same year, distinguish by adding a, b, c etc. to both the text citation and the list of references (e.g. "Smith, 1986a"). References should be collected and typed in alphabetical order after the Notes and Acknowledgements sections (if these exist). Examples:

Benedetti, J. (1988) *Stanislavski*, London: Methuen.

Granville-Barker, H. (1934) Shakespeare's dramatic art. In *A Companion to Shakespeare Studies*, edited by H. Granville-Barker and G.B. Harrison, p. 84. Cambridge: Cambridge University Press.

Johnston, D. (1970) Policy in theatre. *Hibernia*, **16**, 16.

Proofs. Authors will receive page proofs (including figures) by air mail for correction and these must be returned as instructed within 48 hours of receipt. Please ensure that a full postal address is given on the first page of the typescript so that proofs are not delayed in the post. Authors' alterations, other than those of a typographical nature, in excess of 10% of the original composition cost, will be charged to authors.

Page Charges. There are no page charges to individuals or institutions.

INSTRUCTIONS FOR AUTHORS

ARTICLE SUBMISSION ON DISK

The Publisher welcomes submissions on disk. The instructions that follow are intended for use by authors whose articles have been accepted for publication and are in final form. Your adherence to these guidelines will facilitate the processing of your disk by the typesetter. These instructions do not replace the journal Notes for Contributors; all information in Notes for Contributors remains in effect.

When typing your article, do not include design or formatting information. Type all text flush left, unjustified and without hyphenation. Do not use indents, tabs or multi-spacing. If an indent is required, please note it by a line space; also mark the position of the indent on the hard copy manuscript. Indicate the beginning of a new paragraph by typing a line space. Leave one space at the end of a sentence, after a comma or other punctuation mark, and before an opening parenthesis. Be sure not to confuse lower case letter "l" with numeral "1", or capital letter "O" with numeral "0". Distinguish opening quotes from close quotes. Do not use automatic page numbering or running heads.

Tables and displayed equations may have to be rekeyed by the typesetter from your hard copy manuscript. Refer to the journal Notes for Contributors for style for Greek characters, variables, vectors, etc.

Articles prepared on most word processors are acceptable. If you have imported equations and/or scientific symbols into your article from another program, please provide details of the program used and the procedures you followed. If you have used macros that you have created, please include them as well.

You may supply illustrations that are available in an electronic format on a separate disk. Please clearly indicate on the disk the file format and/or program used to produce them, and supply a high-quality hard copy of each illustration as well.

Submit your disk when you submit your final hard copy manuscript. The disk file and hard copy must match exactly.

If you are submitting more than one disk, please number each disk. Please mark each disk with the journal title, author name, abbreviated article title and file names.

Be sure to retain a back-up copy of each disk submitted. Pack your disk carefully to avoid damage in shipping, and submit it with your hard copy manuscript and complete Disk Specifications form (see reverse) to the person designated in the journal Notes for Contributors.

Disk Specifications

Journal name _____

_____

Date _____ **Paper Reference Number** _____

Paper title _____

_____

_____

Corresponding author _____

Address _____

_____

_____

_____ **Postcode** _____

Telephone _____

Fax _____

E-mail _____

Disks Enclosed (file names and descriptions of contents)

Text

Disk 1 _____

Disk 2 _____

Disk 3 _____

PLEASE RETAIN A BACK-UP COPY OF ALL DISK FILES SUBMITTED.

GORDON AND BREACH PUBLISHERS   ●   **HARWOOD ACADEMIC PUBLISHERS**

Figures

Disk 1 _____

Disk 2 _____

Disk 3 _____

Computer make and model _____

_____

Size/format of floppy disks

☐ 3.5"   ☐ 5.25"

☐ Single sided   ☐ Double sided

☐ Single density   ☐ Double density   ☐ High density

Operating system _____

Version _____

Word processor program _____

Version _____

Imported maths/science program _____

Version _____

Graphics program _____

Version _____

Files have been saved in the following format

Text: _____

Figures: _____

Maths: _____

PLEASE RETAIN A BACK-UP COPY OF ALL DISK FILES SUBMITTED.

GORDON AND BREACH PUBLISHERS   ●   **HARWOOD ACADEMIC PUBLISHERS**